for the Benefit of the Public Education Association

April 25—May 12, 1962

PICASSO

an American Tribute

EDITED BY JOHN RICHARDSON

Picasso: An American Tribute

All rights reserved by the Public Education Association

New York, 1962

Catalogue Design by Kathleen Haven

Produced in cooperation with Chanticleer Press, Inc., New York

Printed by Conzett & Huber in Zurich, Switzerland

M. KNOEDLER AND CO., Inc.   1895—1909
14 East 57 Street

SAIDENBERG GALLERY   CUBISM
10 East 77 Street

PAUL ROSENBERG AND CO.   THE TWENTIES
20 East 79 Street

DUVEEN BROTHERS, Inc.   THE CLASSIC PHASE
18 East 79 Street

PERLS GALLERIES   THE THIRTIES
1016 Madison Avenue

STAEMPFLI GALLERY, INC.   THE FORTIES
47 East 77 Street

CORDIER-WARREN GALLERY   THE FIFTIES
978 Madison Avenue

THE NEW GALLERY   DRAWINGS
50 East 78 Street

OTTO GERSON GALLERY   SCULPTURE
41 East 57 Street

Public Education Association 1895–1962

In an address made in 1916, the late Alfred North Whitehead said:

"When one considers in its length and in its breadth the importance of this question of the education of a nation's young, the broken lives, the defeated hopes, the national failures, which result from the frivolous inertia with which it is treated, it is difficult to restrain within oneself a savage rage. In the conditions of modern life the rule is absolute, the race which does not value trained intelligence is doomed. Not all your heroism, not all your social charm, not all your wit, not all your victories on land or at sea, can move back the finger of fate. Today we maintain ourselves. Tomorrow science will have moved forward yet one more step, and there will be no appeal from the judgment which will then be pronounced on the uneducated."

This striking and prophetic statement brings into sharp focus truths which become increasingly evident with each passing year.

The Public Education Association is an independent group of private citizens, supported by membership dues, voluntary contributions and "benefits," which for sixty-eight years has worked steadily and effectively to improve the quality of education provided by the public schools and colleges of New York City. By constant study of the City's huge educational system and its needs; by scrutinizing proposed legislation affecting the schools; by supporting the testing and demonstration of promising new educational practices in close cooperation with school officials and by making accurate information in all of these areas available to the press and to the public, it has provided continuing leadership in the creation of an informed citizenry which can demand for its children, and can get for them, the kind of schools it wants them to have.

Among the reforms which the Public Education Association has initiated, of which many have since been widely adopted by the schools of the entire country, are:

The first School Recreation Program
The first Parent Association
The first Visiting Teachers—now called school social workers
The first Hot Lunch Program
The first Modernization of Teaching Methods
The first School Health Service (including special programs for retarded, cardiac and hard-of-hearing children)
The first "All Day Neighborhood School"
The first School Volunteer Program

The procedure for appointment of members of the Board of Education which had long been advocated by the Association was closely followed by the State Legislature in its action at the Special Session called by the Governor last summer. This has given the City its present excellent, non-political Board of Education.

To the museums and collectors who have most kindly loaned their works of art for this benefit—"Picasso, An American Tribute"—our most grateful thanks. We are equally indebted to the nine cooperating galleries whose generosity has made these exhibitions possible. And to all of you who are helping us in our work for the schools by patronizing this benefit, we want to say that we know you will enjoy these paintings, drawings, and sculptures and we hope you may be interested, also, to ask for a copy of the brief report of September 1961, which describes the Public Education Association. Because each additional member increases the Association's effectiveness in getting a better and better education for our City's young, we hope you may decide to add your strength to ours in this important work by becoming a member.

WILLIAM B. NICHOLS
President

Among the many friends who have made this benefit possible, we wish to express our special gratitude to Mr. Lynn Farnol, Mr. Sampson R. Field, Mrs. Ernest Gillam, Miss Kathleen Haven, Mr. Bryan Holme, Mr. Jan Mitchell, Mr. Douglas Newton, Mr. Robert Rushmore, Mr. Paul Steiner, Mr. Robert Simons and Mr. William Zeckendorf, Jr.

The Public Education Association wishes to express its gratitude to the nine galleries whose cooperation has made this exhibition possible, and to the American museums and collectors who have generously loaned their works of art.

The Allen Memorial Art Museum, Oberlin College
The Art Institute of Chicago
The Baltimore Museum of Art
The Cincinnati Art Museum
The City Art Museum of St. Louis
The Fogg Art Museum, Cambridge
The Solomon R. Guggenheim Museum, New York
The Jewett Arts Center, Wellesley College
The Los Angeles County Museum
The Marion Koogler McNay Art Institute, San Ant
The Metropolitan Museum of Art, New York
The Milwaukee Art Center
The Minneapolis Institute of Arts
The Museum of Modern Art, New York
The Norton Gallery and School of Art, Palm Beach
The Philadelphia Museum of Art
The Phillips Collection, Washington D.C.
The Santa Barbara Museum of Art, California
The Smith College Museum of Art, Northampton
The Virginia Museum of Fine Arts, Richmond
The Wadsworth Atheneum, Hartford
Washington University, St. Louis
The Worcester Art Museum
The Yale University Art Gallery, New Haven

Otto Gerson Gallery, New York
M. Knoedler and Co., Inc., New York
The New Gallery, New York
Perls Galleries, New York
Paul Rosenberg and Co., New York
Saidenberg Gallery, New York
Staempfli Gallery, Inc., New York
E. and A. Silberman Galleries, Inc., New York

America's Tribute to Picasso by John Richardson

"Nine exhibitions: it's unheard of," was Picasso's first reaction on being told about this American tribute to him. *"C'est une blague...* You must be joking ... It's difficult enough to get two galleries to work together, let alone nine." But it did not take long to persuade him that the "triple troika" which the Public Education Association had devised was well on the way to being a reality. The last traces of Picasso's scepticism faded when he started looking through the photographs of each individual exhibition, for photographs of his own works console him in much the same way that photographs of an absent child console a parent. Picasso actively misses pictures that have left his studio: "Now I know where they all go," he said, "to America. I suppose I ought to go after them and see how they are doing ... Your exhibition gives me an excellent excuse. But you know me, I'll never go. I can do all the traveling I want in my head." Picasso spent a long time poring over every work, examining each one as if he had never seen it before, almost as if it were by someone else. Every so often he would make polite, detached comments: "Not bad that one," or "I own one rather like that myself," or "I like the way the pigeon is painted;" and then, half to himself, *"C'est pas si mal la peinture*—better than going to the movies." As usual his highest compliment was to say that a picture was *"vrai;"* when Picasso uses this word, it conveys the quintessence of reality.

As the stacks of photographs which he was looking at diminished, so did Picasso's euphoria. "But it's terrible," he said, "is that *all* you've got to show me? Start work on another nine exhibitions ... Meanwhile let's go through them all again." And he insisted on having a second look at things that had particularly interested him, sometimes in order to identify the subject of a portrait, sometimes to decipher the letters in a cubist still life, sometimes to study a particular group: the pictures of the classical phase, for example, which he enjoyed seeing in isolation. *"Pas si mal,"* he repeated, *"pas si mal ..."*

What never fails to astonish one is the clarity of Picasso's memory. When things interest him, he has almost total recall. For instance, of the first picture in the whole exhibition he said, "The sitter wanted to be taken for an Arab, but he didn't have a burnoose, so I made him wear a terry-cloth robe. I was only fourteen when I painted it." Of the *Bullfight* (Knoedler, No. 6): "Don't imagine that I painted this *after* going to a *corrida.* I did it the day before and sold it so as to have enough money to buy a ticket." Of *The Blue Room* (Knoedler, No. 11): "Uhde got that out of me for thirty francs, the wretch!" Of the *Absinthe Drinker* (Knoedler, No. 18): "Angel de Soto was my best friend in Barcelona. His one desire in life was to please me. You can't imagine how loyal and good-hearted he was ... But he had a horror of work and never did anything except maybe hire a tail-coat and go on as an extra in a musical comedy." Of the *Woman with a Fan* (Knoedler, No. 25): "It's not a portrait, but it was inspired by a girl I noticed in a restaurant. It was really her hat that fascinated me, but in the end I painted it out." Of the *Daniel-Henry Kahnweiler* (Saidenberg, No. 2): "That's just what he looked like... His ears seem to have grown a lot bigger since then. Somewhere I've still got the sculpture that appears in the background—it's from New Caledonia." Of the thickly painted still lifes of 1918 (Rosenberg, Nos. 2 and 4): "One of the pictures in this series—I can't remember which—was painted over a Modigliani; it was wartime and I had run out of canvas." Of the *Still life with Sausage* (Staempfli, No. 4): "It was during the war, and I wanted to do a really gloomy Spanish still life. That's why I made a point of the blackout curtains and painted the forks as if they were souls crying out in purgatory... a real Philip II picture." Of the *Portrait of Dora Maar* (Staempfli, No. 5): "This was originally a portrait of Dora by Cocteau. One day I started to change a detail, but got carried away and repainted the whole thing... Dora's mother had just died, which explains her tense expression." Of the *Femmes d'Alger* (Cordier-Warren, Nos. 6—18): "You know, it's odd, whenever I do a series of pictures, it's usually one of the first two, or one of the last two which I find the best. Here I prefer the one before the last, but most people like the final version." And so Picasso continued, seldom passing over a picture in silence.

When all the photographs had been put away, he said, "I now feel that all these pictures belong to me again. If I go into the studio next door, I wouldn't be surprised to find them stacked against the wall... It's hard to believe that all this and so much more is in America, where I've never been, that so much of me should belong to people I have never even seen... I hardly know any of the collectors, only the X's and the Y's (naming a particularly colorful collector and his wife)—are all the rest of them like that? I hope so." And Picasso proceeded with uncanny skill to mimic their manner of speaking, inventing imaginary English as he went along. "The trouble is one can't know everybody any more. In the old days I knew them all." This led Picasso to reminisce about the Steins who were his first patrons; Alice Toklas whom he still loves, not least because, according to Picasso, she resembles Jacqueline; the Cone sisters, whom he always called the "Miss Etta Cones;" John Quinn whom he advised to buy "Douanier" Rousseau's *Sleeping Gypsy* (now in the Museum of Modern Art); Scott Fitzgerald who amused him; Dr. Barnes who bought some drawings which Picasso refused to sign; Mary Callery whose coiffure was so attractive that he could not resist drawing the back of her head; Alfred and Marga Barr who, he complains, do not come often enough to see him; Dave Duncan who comes all the time; Gary Cooper who gave him a revolver but was unable to hit anything with it; an American sailor who could not wait to sell the portrait Picasso had just done of him, and many more. It was through Gertrude Stein that he came to know and like Americans. "They are not men, they are not women, they are Americans," he told her. "They have done a lot for me," he says.

And when one comes to think of it, Americans have done a lot for Picasso; what is more, their efforts date back well over fifty years. The Steins were the first people to put together a great collection of Picassos; they also persuaded their friends to buy pictures. Other pioneers were Stieglitz and Steichen, who gave Picasso one of his first one-man shows anywhere, in 1911 at the *291* Gallery in New York. Nor were all the critical reactions to this historical exhibition as foolish and philistine as one might have expected. True, Arthur Hoeber of the *New York Globe* described Picasso's austere cubist drawings as "the craziest emanations of a disordered mind, the gibberings of a lunatic." But the *Evening World* critic found that the Picasso of the blue period could "draw and paint with the consummately beautiful mastery of a Millet or a Degas" and that even in "the weird geometrical jumbles . . . there must surely be something doing of large impact for the future." While the *New York World* described the works as "a new thrill in town in the world of art," and the *Newark Evening News,* as extremely interesting experiments that "no one who purposes to keep in touch with the flux of current thought and the currents of the time can . . . afford to ignore." Neither did James Huneker of the *New York Sun* really understand Picasso's art ("His ideal form is pyramidal. There is the back of a giantess corseted. The lines are pyramidal . . . Obsessed by the Egyptians, Picasso has deserted his earlier linear suavity for a hieratic rigidity."), but he wrote a long and sympathetic piece about it.

Three years later, a rather more serious defender of Picasso appeared on the scene: Arthur Jerome Eddy, who in 1914 published a well-argued book, *Cubists and Post-Impressionism,* that had a considerable influence. Meanwhile John Quinn had started to buy Picassos on a big scale, so much so that he owned more than fifty works at his death in 1924. Dr. Barnes also began to amass Picassos around the time of the first war, but his taste was so hamstrung by prejudice—for instance, he accused Picasso of "having fun with the public" in his cubist works—that he acquired very few works painted after 1907. More open-minded were collectors like Walter Arensberg, who started to assemble his magnificent group of Picassos around 1920, A. E. Gallatin, who not only bought for himself but encouraged friends to go after important examples of Picasso's work, and Miss Lillie Bliss, who purchased several pictures at the Quinn sale. By the early twenties, however, collecting Picassos no longer required the courage and artistic perception that it had ten years before. When, in 1923, Paul Rosenberg put on an exhibition of Picasso's neo-classic works at the old Wildenstein Galleries on Fifth Avenue, most of the critics agreed that Picasso had "arrived."

During the late twenties and thirties more works by Picasso were bought by collectors and museums in the United States than in any other country. The impetus for this ever-growing cult of Picasso came almost entirely from one man: Alfred Barr. The great retrospectives that he arranged at the Museum of Modern Art in 1939 and 1956, the exemplary monograph-cum-catalogues that he published on these occasions, and the wonderfully rich corpus of Picasso's work in all media that he built up at the Museum of Modern Art did more for Picasso's renown, internationally as well as nationally, than anybody else's contributions. Mr. Barr was also lucky in having a group of adventurous collectors whose taste he could help to form; and these collectors were in turn lucky in having a group of enterprising and informed dealers—particularly the late Curt Valentin—to supply them with pictures of the quality that they required. It is, therefore, not surprising that the last fifteen years have seen the creation—not only in New York but all over America—of a number of first-rate collections devoted to twentieth century art, many of them with a particular emphasis on Picasso.

Although Picasso has never visited the United States, he has followed the development of American interest in his work with considerable attention. Where else in the world is his fame so generally acknowledged? He does not of course always know which picture is to be found where, but he often has a good idea, and his retentive memory contains a surprising amount of information about the predilections of collectors whom he only knows by name ("Why is it," he will ask, "that the Z's always pick the picture that I would pick myself?"). He is also remarkably well informed about the activities of museum directors and dealers, many of them friends of long standing. Picasso has, therefore, a very clear idea of what these nine exhibitions represent. For him it is not just another retrospective, but a *témoignage d'affection* on the part of known and unknown friends. This birthday present it the more acceptable for the help it gives to children—and children have always been close to the artist's heart. Picasso is also delighted, for once, to be on the receiving and not on the lending end of an exhibition. "I have enough trouble painting my pictures," he said recently, "without wanting the bother of exhibiting them. It makes me feel like a man who has had all the effort of bringing up his daughters and then has to face the complicated business of marrying them off."

Acknowledgments

While preparing this catalogue, I have been fortunate in having the support and encouragement of Monsieur and Madame Picasso. The artist was good enough to look through photographs of all the works that we are exhibiting and to help me with dates and other problems. Monsieur Daniel-Henry Kahnweiler, Picasso's old friend and dealer, was likewise kind enough to give me the benefit of his advice and knowledge on numerous points. I also owe a debt of gratitude to Sir Anthony Blunt, K.C.V.O., who allowed me to work in the Courtauld Institute, London, and to Mr. John Cooper who helped me with research.

Above all I would like to thank Mrs. Victor Ganz for her unflagging assistance and moral support. Without her and without Miss Kathleen Haven, who designed the book and who has been responsible for a great deal of liaison work, this catalogue would never have reached the printers. Mr. William S. Lieberman of the Museum of Modern Art deserves particular thanks for many services, and I am grateful to Miss Jane Sabersky for all kinds of assistance. Special thanks are also due to the nine galleries who have worked together in a unique spirit of cooperation. Everyone associated with them has been unfailingly patient and helpful.

The books and catalogues I have drawn on are too numerous to mention. However, I would like to acknowledge my indebtedness to the Zervos catalogue, Alfred H. Barr's *Picasso: Fifty Years of His Art,* D-H. Kahnweiler's *Sculptures de Picasso,* Roland Penrose's *Picasso: His Life and Work,* Douglas Cooper's *Carnet Catalan* and other publications, John Golding's *Cubism,* Maurice Jardot's Catalogue, *Picasso, 1900—1955* (Paris, 1955), and Dr. Phoebe Pool's as yet unpublished thesis on the literary background to Picasso's early work.

J. R.

M. KNOEDLER and Co., Inc.

1895–1909

Although born at Malaga in the south of Spain, Picasso was fortunate that nine of his most formative years (1895–1904) were spent in Barcelona, the most progressive and independent of Spanish cities. In the 1890's, the city was in a state of artistic florescence. Thanks to the architect, Gaudi, it had become a hotbed of *art nouveau* activity. It had also produced a volatile group of poets, writers and artists who prided themselves on their anarchistic views, peculiar brand of *fin de siècle* decadence and familiarity with the latest trends. One of their beliefs, particularly relevant to Picasso's development, was that the twentieth century would see the dawn of a glorious new art and the emergence of a new type of artist—a Nietzschean superman with a "Dionysiac style." According to those who knew him, Picasso was impressed by Nietzsche's theories. Perhaps he consciously tried to live up to this ideal.

Another peculiarity of the Barcelona artists was a *mystique* for the "Gothic North." By this they meant northern aestheticism: the pre-Raphaelites, Whistler, Beardsley, Böcklin and Heinrich Vogeler. That Picasso shared this enthusiasm emerges in many early pictures. He was also familiar, through reproductions, with a few French artists: Daumier, Carrière, Redon, Toulouse-Lautrec and Steinlen. And as an assiduous visitor to museums, he knew and admired the Spanish masters. His feelings for contemporary Spanish artists, on the other hand, were mixed. For instance, his portraits (Nos. 2 and 3) in the manner of the fashionable local painter Ramón Casas, were done less out of admiration for Barcelona's leading artist than from a desire to prove that he, Picasso, could improve on the same formula.

By 1900, Picasso found Barcelona provincial and confining; he also felt the need to develop a style that would measure up to his technical virtuosity and express his passionate and revolutionary ideas. In quest of this he set off for Paris, a city which conquered him as later he was to conquer it, and which in 1904 became his permanent home. Thanks to his powers of assimilation, the nineteen-year-old artist soon managed to acquaint himself with the latest developments in French art. The Impressionists, Steinlen, Toulouse-Lautrec, Van Gogh, Gauguin, the "Nabis," all had something different to offer him. He also devoured everything that he saw in the Louvre. This artistic gorging resulted in a succession of violent oscillations in style and subject (1900–1901). Picasso first lightened his palette, then brightened it and ultimately allowed it to become pervaded by the color blue. He tried Impressionist brushwork, then a divisionist technique and finally composed his pictures out of simplified silhouettes like Gauguin. He found subjects first in fashionable circles (No. 10), then in *quartiers populaires* and finally in the poorhouse (No. 13) or the gutter. These changes were not always dictated by artistic considerations; they also reflect the rise and fall in the artist's fortunes.

"All that was just sentiment—" Picasso's dismissal his early (pre-1905) work is not without justification. T mannerisms tend to be contrived and the atmosphere theatrical in a Maeterlinckian way. Moreover, despite Picso's atheism, a disagreable element of Spanish religios seeps into some of these pictures: are not the wanderi *saltimbanques*, forlorn mothers and blind beggars in f the Holy Families, Madonnas, and martyrs of Spani seventeenth century art thinly disguised? But when they closest to life, as in the portraits (Nos. 16, 18, and 19), th paintings have a convincing humanity and intensity tl transcend their faults.

The poverty and misery that is such a feature of bl period pictures begin to abate in 1904. Picasso had scrap together enough money to leave Barcelona and settle Paris in a studio in the *Bateau Lavoir*. He had fallen in lc with Fernande Olivier, his companion for the next sev years; he had made a number of stimulating friends; a he was able to sell an occasional picture. The atmosphere his painting lightened accordingly. Blue gives way to pi and Spanish gloom to French nostalgia, as in the series acrobats and carnival people (1905). The artist had ori nally intended to devote three large figure compositions these themes, but only one, *Les Bateleurs,* was ever e: cuted. (No. 22 is a sketch for one of these projects; No. relates to the other). These works reveal that Picasso w temporarily influenced by the Brothers Le Nain, by the cl sical tradition, e.g., the *Boy Leading a Horse* (No. 23), a by Egyptian art, e.g., the hieratic pose of the *Woman w a Fan* (No. 25). But this return to classical and ancient represents a link rather than a break with tradition.

1906 was Picasso's *annus mirabilis*. Accompanied Fernande, he left Paris in June for Gosol (Pyrenee where he spent the summer working mostly on heads a figures (Nos. 27 and 30) that resemble Fernande. Influenc by Iberian sculpture, his style toughened and became mc sculptural and expressive. Back in Paris, he spent the w: ter 1906–07 trying out his new style and finally, in t spring, embarked on a vast figure composition, the *L moiselles d'Avignon,* which he finished in the early su mer. Here at last was the synthesis towards which Picas: had been feeling his way. Iberian sculpture, negro a Cézanne, Gauguin and other influences had been fus by the power of the artist's imagination into a style tl was personal, revolutionary and expressive. At once a n kind of conceptual, as opposed to perceptual, approach art became possible. No less important, the *Demoisel d'Avignon* showed Picasso the way toward the notation form which came to be known as cubism and which tra: formed the art of the twentieth century.

2

1. *Man in a Cowl*. Corunna, 1895. Oil on canvas, 17 × 10″. Private collection.
   This, one of Picasso's earliest portraits, depicts the natural son of Don Ramon Perez Costales, Minister of Education in the first Spanish Republican government (1873—74), and a close friend and neighbor of the artist's father.

2. *By Lamp Light*. Barcelona, 1898. Oil on canvas, 39 × 24¹/₂″. Mr. and Mrs. Monroe Geller, New York.
   A portrait of Cardona, proprietor of a corset shop called "El Stile," whose premises Picasso sometimes used as a studio.

1

3   4

3. *Lola, the Artist's Sister*. Barcelona, 1899. Oil on canvas, 18³⁄₈ × 14³⁄₄″. Jane Taft Ingalls, Cleveland.

4. *The Plumed Hat*. Barcelona, 1900. Oil on canvas, 18³⁄₄ × 15¹⁄₈″. Marion Koogler McNay Art Institute, San Antonio.

5. *Young Girl with Red Flower*. Paris, 1901. Oil on cardboard, 22 × 14″. Mr. and Mrs. Jacques Gelman.

5

6

Bullfight. Barcelona, 1900. Pastel and gouache, 18 × 27″. Mr. and Mrs. Henry J. Heinz II, New York.

Spanish Dancer. 1901. Oil on cardboard, 19¹/₂ × 13³/₈″. Mr. and Mrs. Richard Rodgers, New York.

Absinthe Drinker. Paris, 1901. Oil on canvas, 25³/₄ × 20″. Mr. and Mrs. William B. Jaffe, New York.

7

8

10

11

9. *Boulevard de Clichy*. Paris, 1901. Oil on can[vas],
21½ × 18¼". Mrs. William S. Farish, New York.

10. *Women at Auteuil Races*. Paris, 1901. Oil on can[vas],
17¾ × 23⅝". Mr. and Mrs Joseph H. Hazen, [New]
York.

11. *The Blue Room*. Paris, 1901. Oil on can[vas],
20 × 24½". The Phillips Collection, Washing[ton],
D.C.

12

13

Café Scene. Barcelona 1902, Pastel, 12 × 15¼".
Mr. and Mrs. Lee A. Ault, New York.

Blind Man's Meal. Barcelona, 1903. Oil on canvas,
37½ × 37½". The Metropolitan Museum of Art,
New York (Gift of Mr. and Mrs. Ira Haupt. 1950).
The Barnes Foundation owns a letter from Picasso
written when he was working on this picture. Besides giving a sketch of the composition, which
originally included a dog in the bottom left corner,
he writes: "I am doing a blind man seated at a
table; he has a piece of bread in his left hand and
with his right he gropes for his jug of wine. At his
side is a dog which looks at him. I am quite
pleased. It's still not finished."

14. *Mother and Child at the Seashore*. Barcelona, 1902.
Oil on canvas, 32³/₄ × 23³/₄″. Private collection.

15

15. *Harlequin*. Paris, 1901. Oil on canvas, $32^5/_8 \times 24^1/_8''$.
The Metropolitan Museum of Art, New York (Gift
of Mr. and Mrs. John L. Loeb. 1960).

16. *At the "Lapin Agile."* Paris, 1904. Oil on canvas, 39 × 39¹/₂". Mr. and Mrs. Charles S. Payson, New York.

The harlequin figure is a self-portrait. And, according to Picasso, the figure of the girl is a likeness of Germaine for whom his great friend, the painter Casagemas, committed suicide. In the background is Frédé, proprietor of the "Lapin Agile," at this period the favorite rendezvous of the Montmartre artists, but soon to become a tourist trap.

17

17. *Chrysanthemums*. Barcelona, 1903. Oil on canvas, 32 × 25³/₄″. M. Knoedler and Co., Inc., New York.

18. *The Absinthe Drinker*. Barcelona, 1903. Oil on canvas, 27¹/₂ × 21³/₄″. Mr. and Mrs. Donald S. Stralem, New York.
    A portrait of Angel Fernandez de Soto, Picasso's closest friend in Barcelona. A ne'er-do-well of great charm and kindness, he frequently shared his quarters with Picasso. He was killed in a street accident in the 1930's.

19. *Madame Soler*. Barcelona, 1903. Oil on canvas, 39³/₈ × 27¹/₂″. Thannhauser Foundation, New York.
    Madam Soler's husband was a Barcelona tailor who made Picasso's suits in exchange for portraits of himself and his family.

18

19

20

20. *Meditation*. Paris, 1904. Pen and watercolor,
13³/₄ × 10¹/₈″. Mrs. Bertram Smith, New York.
The figure on the right is a self-portrait. This is one
of the first manifestations of the "sleeper watched"
theme which recurs throughout Picasso's work.

21. *Circus Family*. Paris, 1905. Pen and watercolor,
9¹/₂ × 12″. The Baltimore Museum of Art (The
Cone Collection).
A project for one of three large *Saltimbanque*
compositions, only one of which *(Les Bateleurs:*
Chester Dale Collection, National Gallery of Art,
Washington) was ever executed. The figure in the
right foreground recurs in the *Acrobat on a Ball*
(Museum of Modern Western Art, Moscow).

22. *The Harlequin's Family*. Paris, 1905. Ink and
gouache, 23 × 17¹/₄″. Mr. and Mrs. Julian C. Eisen-
stein, Washington, D.C.

22

23

23. *Boy Leading a Horse.* Paris, 1905. Oil on canvas,
     87 × 51¼″. Mr. and Mrs. William S. Paley, New
     York.

24

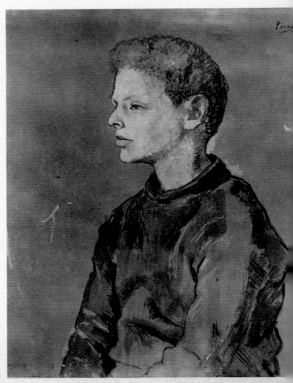

24. *Boy with Collar.* Paris, 1905. Gouache on cardboard, 31¼ × 23½″. Worcester Art Museum (The Dial Collection).

25. *Woman with a Fan.* Paris, 1905. Oil on canvas, 39½ × 32″. The Hon. and Mrs. W. Averell Harriman, New York.

26. *Portrait of Allan Stein.* Paris, early 1906. Gouache on cardboard, 29⅛ × 23½″. The Baltimore Museum of Art (The Cone Collection).
The sitter (1895–1951) was the son of Gertrude Stein's brother, Michael.

27

28

29

27. *Woman with Kerchief.* Gosol, summer 1906. Gouache and charcoal, 26 × 19¹/₂″. The Virginia Museum of Fine Arts, Richmond (T. Catesby Jones Collection).

28. *Portrait of Fernande Olivier.* Paris, summer 1906. Oil on canvas, 39³/₈ × 31⁷/₈″. The Solomon Trust, Cambridge, Mass.
    Fernande Olivier was the artist's companion from 1903 until 1911, during which period she became a talented amateur painter. Her works, of which Picasso owns a large collection, are in the manner of Marie Laurencin but more robust. She left Picasso for the Italian painter, Oppi, but soon went to live with Roger Karl, one of the first French film stars.

29. *Head of a Woman.* Paris, summer 1906. Gouache, 24¹/₂ × 18¹/₄″. Private collection.

30   31

32

30. *Head of a Boy*. Gosol, summer 1906. Gouache
cardboard, 15 × 10″. Mr. and Mrs. Lee A. Ault, ⬛
York.

31. *Head of a Boy*. Paris, late 1906. Oil on can⬛
14 × 9″. Madame Helena Rubinstein, New York

32. *Head of a Woman*. Paris, summer 1906. Oi⬛
canvas, 14³/₄ × 13″. Private collection.

33

Woman in Yellow. Paris, summer 1907. Oil on canvas, 51¼ × 37⅜″. Mr. and Mrs. Joseph Pulitzer, Jr., St. Louis.

Vase of Flowers. Paris, summer 1907. Oil on canvas, 36½ × 28½″. Mr. and Mrs. Ralph F. Colin, New York.

35

35. *Seated Woman*. Paris, early 1908. Oil on canvas, 28³/₄ × 23¹/₂″. Mr. Larry Aldrich, New York.

36. *Studies of Man's Head*. Paris, 1908. Gouache and pencil, 12¹/₂ × 9¹/₂″. Jewett Arts Center, Wellesley College, Mass.

37. *Nude with Raised Arm (Study for "Nude with Drapery")*. Paris, summer 1907. Ink, wash and watercolor, 12¹/₄ × 9¹/₂″. The Baltimore Museum of Art (The Cone Collection).

38. *Still Life with Flowers*. La-Rue-des-Bois, autumn, 1908. Oil on canvas, 15 × 18¹/₄″. Mr. and Mrs. Peter A. Rübel, New York.

39. *Female Nude*. Paris, winter 1908. Oil on canvas, 45³/₄ × 35″. Philadelphia Museum of Art (The Louise and Walter Arensberg Collection).

37

38

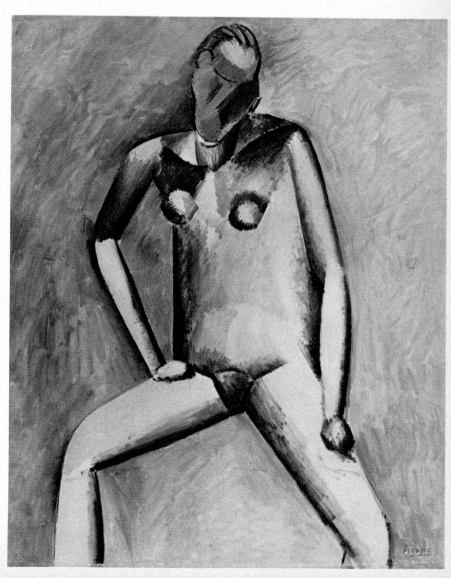

39

40

40. *Harlequin*. Paris, spring 1909. Oil on can[vas,]
36½ × 28½". Mr. Enrico Donati, New York.

41. *Head of a Youth*. 1909. Oil on canvas, 25 × 1[6"?]
Mr. and Mrs. William A. Bernoudy, St. Louis.

42

43

Portrait of Manuel Pallarés. Horta de San Juan, summer 1909. Oil on canvas, 26³/₄ × 19¹/₂″. Saidenberg Gallery, New York.

Manuel Pallarés, still a close friend of Picasso's, was a painter whose family owned a property at Horta de San Juan, a village in the Ebro valley, which Picasso visited in 1898 and again at this crucial moment in his development.

Seated Nude. Paris, late 1909. Oil on canvas, 31⁷/₈ × 25⁵/₈″. Perls Galleries, New York.

44. *Portrait of Braque*. Paris, late 1909. Oil on canvas, 24¼ × 19¾". Mr. Edward A. Bragaline, New York. Braque did not sit for this "portrait" and says that it was never a real likeness, but simply the head of a man slightly resembling him and wearing a hat known as a "Kronstadt."

SAIDENBERG GALLERY

Cubism

Cubism has been the most influential art movement of the twentieth century, yet many people are still baffled by it. It was never an artistic theory or method or a magic, picture-making formula as some artists hoped, but a new pictorial means of representing form and space and re-creating the reality of things. Cubism was constantly subject to modification, because Picasso and Braque—its two creators—were intuitive as opposed to scientific in their approach. All that they had to guide them were the pioneer discoveries of Cézanne, and these they soon outstripped. Every other tenet of art they questioned and usually condemned: the notion of a single viewpoint, tonal values, chiaroscuro and, above all, perspective, which they denounced as an eye-fooling trick. "We wanted to paint not what you *see* but what you *know* is there," said Picasso many years later.

The progress of the movement was startlingly rapid, but inevitably there were times when one painter or the other was confronted with an apparently insoluble problem. Such a time for Picasso was the summer of 1910, the date of the first picture in this exhibition. With Derain and Fernande Olivier, Picasso had gone to spend the summer at Cadaqués on the Costa Brava. He embarked on some impressive, if hermetic, figure paintings, but he began to find them increasingly difficult to resolve. The more he concentrated on creating a formal and spatial element, the more he lost touch with visual facts. *The Rower* (No. 1)— a typical product of the Cadaqués period in that it is hermetic to the point of being indecipherable—reveals this dilemma. A step further, and Picasso would have turned into a nonfigurative painter. This he shrank from doing, for his art could only flourish if it had its roots deep in what he felt to be reality.

When he returned to Paris in the autumn of 1910, Picasso's paintings became more legible. He provided basic descriptive indications without sacrificing formal and spatial considerations. The improvement can be seen in the *Dressing Table* (No. 3), in which the objects fuse with the space around them but do not lose their identities. Likewise, the *Portrait of Kahnweiler* (No. 2) retains a necessary element of likeness, even though the figure and the setting form a single, faceted mass.

In 1911 Picasso, like Braque, continued to break down appearances analytically into component parts, fragmenting and faceting their forms, then fusing them together into a more homogeneous and pictorially more meaningful whole. This can be followed in a series of remarkable still lifes and monumental figure paintings which are among the glories of cubism. By the spring of 1912, both artists realized that there were still many problems. How, for instance, could they simplify their method of notation? And what could they do about color, the one element they had fought shy of?

At this crucial juncture (June 1912), the Braques joi Picasso at Sorgues, a village near Avignon; there t embarked on a series of experiments. They made elabo constructions of cardboard and paper; mixed sand, wo shavings, metal filings, tobacco, soot and even ashes v their pigment in an attempt to equate color with textu and tried out decorator's effects—marbleizing, letter stenciling and wood-graining. But these were only par solutions to the problem of how to bring color into th pictures. Braque suddenly realized that Picasso had b on the right track, six months earlier, when he had in duced a piece of oil-cloth into a still life; he saw hov exploit this and, in September 1912, started to introd wallpaper and newspaper into his compositions—a prac that Picasso also adopted.

The technique of pasted paper enabled the artis represent an object by some foreign element that was equivalent of itself (a piece of newspaper, for instance, l piece of newspaper), and to use drawing simultaneo and independently to indicate the separate function volume. This opened the door to a new range of tac effects, injected an extra measure of reality into art, est lished the artist's right to incorporate the humblest m rials into his pictures and abolished the frontier betw sculpture and painting by making possible the *table objet*. Most far reaching of all, it changed the whole cou of cubist and post-cubist painting by revealing that artist, instead of breaking down reality *analytically* int component parts, could just as well reverse the process reconstruct reality *synthetically* out of elements that v not in themselves representational. This new appro manifests itself in such pictures as Nos. 17 and 18, wl the composition is built up out of flat, colored or patter planes which simulate pasted papers. These enabled artist to conjure up a formal or spatial element with violating the flatness of the picture surface.

From 1909 until 1914 cubism must be seen as a j venture on the part of Picasso and Braque. When began, this partnership, unique in the history of art, br up and was never resumed. Picasso returned to Paris continued to exploit synthetic cubist discoveries i series of attractive, often brilliant pictures whose c shortcomings are a certain coldness and decorativen Exception, however, must be made for a few paintings No. 26, which have the intensity of earlier works and t mysterious pictorial reality which transcends the realit actual objects.

In 1915 Picasso shocked his followers by produc the first of his Ingresque portraits—a deliberately a cubist gesture. Picasso did not, however, abandon cubi Between 1916 and 1926 he painted a number of magiste still lifes in this idiom, and in subsequent periods continued to profit from his cubist discoveries.

1. *The Rower*. Cadaqués, summer 1910. Oil on canvas, 28³/₈ × 23³/₈″. Mr. and Mrs. Ralph F. Colin, New York.

2

3

2. *Daniel-Henry Kahnweiler*. Paris, autumn 1910. O
   canvas, 39⅝ × 28⅝″. The Art Institute of Chi
   (Gift of Mrs. Gilbert W. Chapman).
   The configuration in the top left-hand corner r
   sents a piece of sculpture from New Caledonia
   Picasso had in his studio when he painted
   portrait.

3. *The Dressing Table*. Paris, 1910. Oil on ca
   24 × 18″. Mr. and Mrs. Ralph F. Colin, New Yo

4. *Still Life with Pipe-Rack, Cup, Coffee Pot and*
   rafe. Paris, winter 1910–11. Oil on ca
   19⅞ × 50¼″. Perls Galleries, New York.
   The letters "La Aux Dumas" refer to *"La Dame*
   Camélias" by Dumas. Picasso shared with A
   naire a cult for the heroine of this book.

5. *The Accordionist*. Céret, summer 1911. Oil on
   vas, 51¼ × 35¼″. The Solomon R. Guggen
   Museum, New York.

6. *The Glass of Absinthe*. 1911. Oil on ca
   15⅛ × 18¼″. Allen Memorial Art Museum, Ob
   College.

4

6

5

7

8

9

7. *Still Life ("Notre Avenir est dans l'Air")*. Paris, spring 1912. Oil on canvas. 15 × 21³/₄″. E. and A. Silberman Galleries, Inc., New York.
   "Notre Avenir est dans l'Air" (Our future is in the air) was the title of a brochure on aviation published in 1912. The ideas expressed in it became an obsession with Picasso, as witness this and two other still lifes of the same date.

8. *The Carafe*. Paris, winter 1911—12. Oil on canvas, 8¹/₂ × 6″. M. Knoedler and Co., Inc., New York.

9. *Figure*. Paris, 1913. Ink, charcoal and pasted papers, 18 × 14″. Madame Helena Rubinstein, New York.

10. *The Model*. Sorgues, spring 1912. Oil on canvas, 45³/₄ × 32″. Dr. Herschel Carey Walker, New York.

11. *Man with Guitar*. Sorgues, summer 1912 — Paris, spring 1913. Oil on canvas, 51⁷/₈ × 35″. Philadelphia Museum of Art (The Louise and Walter Arensberg Collection).

10   11

12. *The Violin*. Paris, winter 1912–13. Charcoal, watercolor and pasted papers, 24³/₄ × 19″. The New Gallery, New York.

13. *Guitar and Wine Glass*. 1913. Charcoal, gou[a] and pasted papers, 18⁷/₈ × 14³/₈″. Marion Koo McNay Art Institute, San Antonio.

12

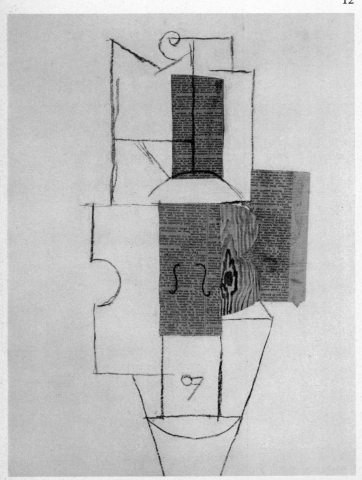

14

15

Stuffed Bird on a Branch. Paris, late 1913. Oil on canvas, 13 × 5⁷/₈″. Private collection, New York.

Head of a Man. Paris, spring 1913. Oil, charcoal, ink and pencil on sized paper, 24¹/₄ × 18¹/₄″. Mr. Richard S. Zeisler, New York.

Guitar and Bottle of Bass. Paris, 1913. Charcoal and gouache, 10 × 9³/₄″. Madame Pierre Chareau, New York.

16

17. *Glass and Bottle of Bass on a Table*. Paris, 1913. Charcoal, pasted papers and sawdust cardboard, 29 × 22″. Mr. and Mrs. George He Warren, New York.

18. *The Guitar*. Paris, late 1913. Oil and sand on vas, 45³/₄ × 32″. Mr. and Mrs. George Henry V ren, New York.

17

19

19. *The Fruit Dish.* Céret, spring 1912. Oil on canvas,
    21³/₄ × 15″. Private Collection, New York.
    The letters "Zagra" refer to *Mazagram,* a popular
    brand of coffee, "Re" to Céret, where this picture
    was painted, and "Hotel Du" to the Hotel Duedra,
    where Picasso stayed.

20. *Still Life with Playing Cards, Glasses and Bottle of Rum ("Vive la...").* Avignon, summer 1914—Paris, 1915. Oil and sand on canvas, 21³/₈ × 25³/₄". Mr. and Mrs. Leigh B. Block, Chicago.

21

21. *Guitar and Sheet Music ("Ma Jolie")*. Paris, winter 1913—14. Oil on canvas, $17^{1}/_{2} \times 16''$. Mr. and Mrs. Lee A. Ault, New York.

"Ma Jolie" is at the same time a reference to a popular song, *"O Manon, ma jolie, mon cœur te dit bonjour,"* and a tribute to the charms of Marcelle Humbert (rechristened "Eva" by Picasso), who was the artist's companion from 1912 until her early death at the end of 1915. "I love her very much," Picasso wrote Kahnweiler (12 June 1912), "and I shall write her name on my pictures." Oblique references like this are the closest Picasso came to doing a portrait of her.

22

Still Life with Grapes, Pear and Newspaper on a Table. Avignon, summer 1914. Oil and sand on canvas, $5^{1}/_{8} \times 6^{1}/_{4}''$. M. Knoedler and Co., Inc., New York.

23

23. *Still Life with Glass and Playing Card ("Homage to Max Jacob")*. Paris, 1914. Charcoal, gouache and pasted papers on cardboard, $14 \times 18''$. E. E. W. Collection, New York.

24. *Still Life with Aeroplane*. Paris, 1915. Pencil and watercolor, 7¹/₂ × 6″. Private collection, New York.

25. *Guitar on Table*. Paris, 1915. Pencil and watercolor, 5³/₄ × 4³/₄″. Private collection, New York.

26. *Woman Seated in Armchair*. Paris, 1915. Pencil and watercolor, 9¹/₂ × 7¹/₂″. Private collection, New York.

24

25

26

Grapes and Bottle on Table ("Job"). Paris, 1916.
Oil and sand on canvas, 17 × 13¹/₄″. Private collection, New York.
"Job" is the name of a brand of French cigarette
papers, a packet of which appears on the right.

Italian Girl. Rome, 1917. Watercolor, 29³/₄ × 20¹/₂″.
Paul Rosenberg and Co., New York.
A study for the large painting of the same date
belonging to the Heirs of Herr Emil Bührle, Zürich.

27

28

29

29. *Woman with Fan.* 1910—18. Oil on can
72³/₄ × 28¹/₂″. Mr. and Mrs. Burton Trema
Meriden, Conn.
Begun at the most "hermetic" moment of cub
(*c.f.* No. 1) and left unfinished like many o
works of the period, this picture was not reso
until eight years later, when it was overpai
with a grid of emphatic outlines and the
schematic planes of synthetic cubism. The diffe
approaches to the same pictorial problem
easily distinguishable and point one another u

PAUL ROSENBERG and Co.

The Twenties

This exhibition and the one devoted to the "Classical Phase" at Duveen Brothers represent reverse sides of the same medal. At Duveen's we see the consequences of Picasso's attempt to substitute the example of Ingres for the discipline of cubism. Whereas here—appropriately enough in the gallery founded by Paul Rosenberg, Picasso's dealer and friend for many years—we see how he carried on, during the same period, as a Cubist. So wide is the gulf between the two styles that we are entitled to regard the Picasso of 1920—25 as two separate artists.

The nature of Picasso's stylistic dichotomy is easy to understand if a group of cubist still lifes (Nos. 29—33, for instance) is contrasted with a group of highly modeled figure compositions, such as Nos. 29—33 in the Duveen exhibition. All these works were executed at Dinard during the course of the summer of 1922, but what an enormous difference there is! The more rigorously Picasso flattens forms in his still lifes, the more vigorously he inflates heads and nudes. It may seem paradoxical, but Picasso's motives were the same in the case of both processes. Like most great artists who followed on from Cézanne, he was intent on reconciling two irreconcilables: three-dimensional appearances and the two-dimensional surface of paper or canvas. In his classical figure compositions, Picasso took the traditional course of emphasizing volume; in his synthetic cubist works he made a virtue of flatness. Another difference is that in his classical works Picasso generally seems to be looking backward, sometimes with nostalgia, sometimes with mockery; whereas in synthetic cubist works he tends to be a creative and forward-looking artist. These two sides of his art correspond to the two conflicting aspects of his life at this period: the one temporarily conformist, the other incorrigibly experimental.

The development of this last great period of synthetic cubism can easily be followed through the *Guéridons*— still lifes on a pedestal table, usually in front of an open window—which are a recurrent feature of this exhibition. Picasso had originally toyed with this compositional idea in a drawing (Zervos, Vol. III, No. 11) done when he was living in Montrouge in 1917. But it was not until he returned from the Russian Ballet season in London in the summer of 1919 and went to stay at Saint-Raphaël, that it turns into a dominant theme of his work. Picasso says that he became obsessed by the pattern of the balcony grille outside his bedroom window (he still watches out for it every time he drives through Saint-Raphaël) and ended by incorporating it as a decorative *motif* in a number of still lifes. In the first of these (Nos. 8—11) naturalistic and cubistic elements are cunningly combined. The setting is indicated in a straightforward, representational way, but the still life is a complex construction of flat, interlocking planes, for which a number of analytical drawings and some three-dimensional cardboard models (Zervos, Vol. III, Nos. 414—

15) were made. When he returned to Paris in the autumn Picasso continued to work on the same idea, replacing the Mediterranean with the view from his Paris apartmen (No. 14), or a background of shutters (No. 16). The serie culminated in the grandiose *Table* (No. 13) of 1919—20 which is a kind of abstraction of the original *guéridon* idea From this key work evolved the decorative still lifes con structed out of parallel lines (Nos. 28, 29, 30 and 31) o 1922, which sometimes topple over into decorative callig raphy. Picasso soon rejected this manner and returned t the straightforward flatness of synthetic cubism.

From 1920 until 1925, Picasso reserved his classica style for figures and his synthetic cubist style for still life Exceptions are the numerous gouaches (Nos. 18—22) an occasional paintings of flat, schematic harlequins, also th two versions of the *Three Musicians* (1921) which sum u on a monumental scale the achievements of syntheti cubism. Surprisingly, these do not bring the style to an end As the present exhibition reveals, cubism carried on unt 1925—26, when it culminated in a blaze of brilliant sti lifes. These may be limited in subject but are astor ishingly varied in their dazzling colors, elaborate pa terning, rich textures and complex compositions. No long did Picasso feel obliged to investigate the intricate form and spatial problems that had preoccupied him ten year before. Instead, he felt free to relax and exploit his cubi discoveries in a decorative manner that delights the ey even if it seldom engages the mind. In 1923 he reverts the *Guéridon* theme in some large upright pictures (Nos. and 34), but in 1924 his format is more often a horizont one, as witness such ornate set-pieces as Nos. 24 and 35 works that recall such disparate artists as de Heem ar Matisse, but could only have been painted by Picasso.

Like the best classical pictures of the same date, mc of the paintings on view here reflect the harmony ar serenity of the artist's private life. This was not to la Around the middle of the decade Picasso's style becar what can only be described as expressionistic, even torture as his wife, Olga, grew increasingly jealous and possessiv The end of the period covered by this exhibition is a nounced by the *Danse* (1925), an epoch-making picture which Picasso transforms the flat elegant planes of sy thetic cubism into the distorted images described by t Surrealists—Picasso's new friends—as "convulsive." Ne again did the artist's style recapture the air of magister calm that is such a feature of this last great phase of cubi

Harlequin. Montrouge, 1918. Oil on
canvas, 57³/₄ × 26¹/₄″. Mr. and Mrs.
Joseph Pulitzer, Jr., St. Louis.

2

2. *Pipe, Glass and Tobacco Packet*. Montrouge, 1918. Oil and sand on canvas, 10½ × 13¾″. Private collection, New York.

3. *Tobacco Packet and Pipe*. Montrouge, 1918. Oil on canvas, 8½ × 10¼″. Private collection, New York.

4. *Pipe and Glass,* Montrouge, 1918. Oil and sand on canvas, 10½ × 8½″. Private collection, New York.

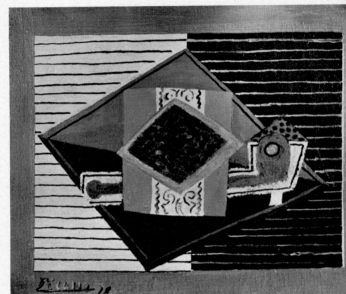

4

5

6

5. *Still Life with Pigeon*. Paris, 1919. Oil on canvas, 10¹/₂ × 13³/₄″. Private collection, New York.

6. *Glass, Pipe and Tobacco Packet*. Paris, 1919. Oil on canvas, 8³/₄ × 6¹/₂″. Private collection, New York.

7. *Glass, Tobacco Packet and Playing Card*. Paris, 1919. Oil on canvas, 7¹/₂ × 10¹/₂″. Private collection, New York.

7

8. *Table in front of Open Window*. Saint Raphaël, summer 1919. Oil on canvas, 8½ × 8½″. Private collection, New York.

9. *Table in front of Open Window*. Saint-Raphaël, summer 1919. Gouache, 13¾ × 9¾″. Private collection, New York.

10. *Table in front of Open Window*. Saint-Rapha summer 1919. Watercolor and gouache, 13 × 8¾/ Mr. and Mrs. Daniel Saidenberg, New York.

11. *Table in front of Open Window*. Saint-Rapha summer 1919. Oil on canvas, 11½ × 9″. Priv. collection, New York.

8

10

9

11

12. *The Table*. Paris, 1919–20. Oil on canvas, 50¼ × 29″. Smith College Museum of Art, Northampton.

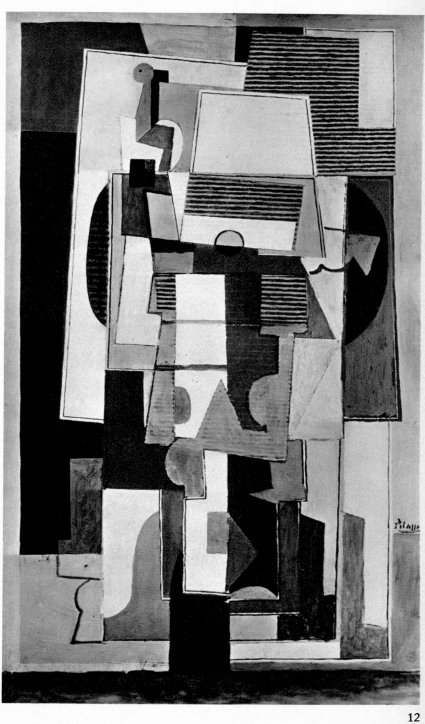

13

14

13. *Table in front of Open Window (rue de Penthièvre).*
Paris, 1920. Oil on canvas, 64¹/₂ × 43″. Private collection, New York.

14. *Table in front of Shuttered Window.* Paris, 1919.
Oil on canvas, 8³/₄ × 5″. Private collection, New
York.

15

15. *Composition with Guitar and Score.* Juan-les-Pins, summer 1920. Gouache, 8¼ × 10½″. Private collection, New York.

16. *Composition with Guitar and Score.* Juan-les-Pins, summer 1920. Gouache, 10½ × 8¼″. Private collection, New York.

17. *Composition with Guitar and Score.* Juan-les-Pins, summer 1920. Gouache, 10½ × 8¼″. Private collection, New York.

16

17

18

18. *Pierrot and Harlequin at a Café Table*. Juan-
Pins, summer 1920. Gouache, 8¹/₄ × 10¹/₂″. Pri
collection, New York.

19. *Pierrot and Harlequin at a Café Table*. Juan-
Pins, summer 1920. Gouache, 8¹/₄ × 10¹/₂″. Pri
collection, New York.

20. *Pierrot and Harlequin at a Café Table*. Juan-
Pins, summer 1920. Gouache, 8¹/₄ × 10¹/₂″. Pri
collection, New York.

21. *Pierrot and Harlequin*. Juan-les-Pins, summer 1
Gouache, 10¹/₂ × 8¹/₄″. Private collection, New Y

22. *Pierrot and Harlequin*. Juan-les-Pins, summer 1
Gouache, 10¹/₂ × 8¹/₄″. Private collection, New Y

20

21

23. *Harlequin with Violin ("Si Tu Veux")*. Montrouge,
    1918. Oil on canvas, 56 × 39½″. Private collection,
    New York.

24. *The Red Tablecloth*. Paris, December 1924. Oil on
canvas, 38³/₄ × 51³/₄″. Private collection, New York.

25

26

25. *Dog and Cock*. 1921. Oil on canvas, 61 × 30¼".
Yale University Art Gallery, New Haven (Gift of
Stephen C. Clark).

26. *Still Life ("Le Jour")*. Paris, 1921. Oil on canvas,
29 × 36½". Mr. and Mrs. Joseph H. Hazen, New
York.

27

28

27. *Glass and Fruit Dish*. Paris, 1922. Oil on canvas, 10¹/₂ × 13³/₄". Private collection, New York.

28. *Mandolin on a Table*. Paris, 1922. Oil on canvas, 32 × 39¹/₂". Mr. and Mrs. William B. Jaffe, New York.

29. *Apple, Glass and Lemon*. Dinard, summer 1⁹ Oil on canvas. 8¹/₂ × 10¹/₂". Private collection, N York.

30. *Glass and Fruit*. Dinard, summer 1922. Oil on c vas, 7¹/₂ × 9¹/₄". Private collection, New York.

Four Fish. Dinard, summer 1922. Oil on canvas, 8¹/₂ × 10¹/₂″. Private collection, New York.

32. *Slice of Fish*. Dinard, summer 1922. Oil on canvas, 8³/₄ × 10¹/₂″. Private collection, New York.

33. *Still Life with Fish*. Dinard, summer 1922—Paris, winter 1923. Oil on canvas, 51 × 38¹/₄″. Mrs. Albert D. Lasker, New York.

34

34. *Guitar and Fruit Dish on Table*. 1924. Oil on c
vas, 51³/₄ × 38³/₄″. Mr. and Mrs. Daniel Saidenb
New York.

35. *Mandolin and Guitar*. Juan-les-Pins, summer 1⁹
Oil and sand on canvas, 56¹/₈ × 79³/₄″. The S
mon R. Guggenheim Museum, New York.

35

36

36. *The Red Foulard.* 1924. Oil on canvas, 39¹/₂ × 32″. Norton Gallery and School of Art, Palm Beach.

37. *Glass of Chocolate and Croissant.* Paris, 1923. Oil on canvas, 7¹/₂ × 9¹/₂″. Private collection, New York.

37

38. *The Bird Cage*. Paris, 1923. Oil on canvas, 79¼ × 55¼″. Private collection, New York.

39. *The Plaster Arm*. Paris, 1925. Oil on can 38¾ × 51¾″. Mr. and Mrs. Samuel Marx, Chic

41. *Harlequin with Guitar*. Paris, 1924. Oil on canvas,
51¼ × 38¼″. Mr. and Mrs. Leigh B. Block, Chicago.

The Breakfast. Paris, 1924. Oil on canvas, 15 × 18″.
Mr. Edward Bragaline, New York.

42. *Still Life with Biscuits*. 1924. Oil and sand on canvas, 32 × 39¾″. Private collection, New York.

43. *Woman with Mandolin*. 1925. Oil on canvas,
51³/₄ × 35³/₄″. Private collection, New York.

44. *The Ram's Head*. Juan-les-Pins, summer 1925. Oil on canvas, 31^1/$_2$ × 39^1/$_2$″. Private collection, New York.

45. *The Net*. Juan-les-Pins, summer 1925. Oil on canvas, 39^3/$_4$ × 32^1/$_2$″. Private collection, New York.

46. *The Bottle of Wine*. Paris, 1925—26. Oil on canvas,
38³/₄ × 51¹/₂″. Private collection, New York.

47. *Harlequin*. Paris, 1927. Oil on canvas, 31³/₄ × 2
Perls Galleries, New York.

DUVEEN BROTHERS, Inc.

The Classical Phase

At certain turning points in his development Picasso has drawn sustenance from his Mediterranean heritage and the classical tradition that reflects it. The vigor of archaic sculpture, the sophistication of Roman marbles, the decorative trappings of Pompeian frescoes, the linear vitality of Greek vases and mirror-backs and the typically Mediterranean combination of pagan gusto and formal orderliness: all this has inspired Picasso at different times. During the blue period, for instance, he looked at classicism through the eyes of Puvis de Chavannes and Gauguin; in 1906—07 he found inspiration for the *Demoiselles d'Avignon* in Iberian sculpture; in the early thirties he followed up the illustrations he had done for Ovid's *Metamorphoses* with numerous engravings and drawings that are classical in theme and style; and in 1945—46, when he was able to return to the Mediterranean, he forgot the misery of the war in light-hearted Bacchanalian scenes. But Picasso's most intensive classical phase was the one that is the subject of this exhibition. It lasted from 1918 until 1924 and coincides, significantly enough, with Picasso's first period of friendship with Jean Cocteau, his connection with the Diaghilev ballet and the early years of his marriage.

Probably the most decisive of these factors was the artist's marriage in 1918 to Olga Koklova, a beautiful but conventionally-minded ballet dancer who was determined to transform her husband from a *farouche* Bohemian into a chic and worldly gentleman. The couple moved into a large new apartment on the rue de la Boétie, where Picasso evolved the mannered and sophisticated style which permeates the pictures in this exhibition. Supporters of cubism were dismayed by their leader's defection, but Jean Cocteau—for a brief period the catalyst in Picasso's life—approved, as he too was preaching a return to the classical tradition which, he claimed, was much more avant garde than most of what passed for modernity. As with Cocteau, Picasso's traditionalism contained a deliberate element of perversity and mockery—hardly surprising in someone who has always enjoyed poking fun at canons of beauty. On the other hand, the best of Picasso's classical pictures are informed with artistic seriousness and human feeling, for instance the life-size *Pipes of Pan* (1923), which the artist considers the masterpiece of his classical period and has kept for himself, or the *Maternity* paintings (Nos. 15—18), which reflect his pride and happiness at the birth of his son in February 1921. So long as domestic harmony lasted, the classical style prevailed. But the minute Picasso began to feel stifled by the Parisian social round and Russian domesticity, classicism gave way to a more tortured—and in many ways more interesting—style, the first intimations of which appear in the frenetic *Dance* (1925). Picasso says that at this point he wanted to put a notice on his studio door inscribed: *"Je ne suis pas un gentleman."*

Picasso's classical phase must also be seen as a reaction against cubism—a reaction that was triggered partly by disgust at the way second-rate artists were trying to turn his and Braque's discoveries into a picture-making formula, partly by technical curiosity and restlessness. The consequence is an odd bifurcation in Picasso's artistic personality. Instead of making a clean break with the past, he continued to work simultaneously in a synthetic cubist idiom (as witness pictures in the Saidenberg and Rosenberg exhibitions) as well as in a more academic manner. This academicism first manifests itself in the Ingresque portraits of Vollard, Max Jacob and Léonce Rosenberg of 1915, and in the drawings (unpublished) of his mistress, Gaby Lespinasse (1916), which recall the neo-classical manner of Renoir. "I wanted to show that I could draw like anybody else," Picasso said, but he also wanted to give an airing to the academic virtuoso that lurks within him. Picasso's classical tendency received further encouragement in 1917 when he went to work with Diaghilev in Italy. Rome was a revelation, and the marbles and Pompeian frescoes that he saw in Naples showed him the way towards the new style that we see in these pictures.

So completely did Picasso digest and transform classical influences that it is difficult to relate specific compositions to this or that classical original. Exceptions are the life-size *Three Graces,* based on the famous Greek prototype, and a drawing of a woman with her hand to her face (Zervos, Vol. IV, No. 50), which corresponds to Ingres' *Madame Moitessier* and to the figure in the *Herakles and Telephus* fresco (National Museum, Naples) that is generally thought to have inspired the Ingres. At this period Picasso was also influenced by French eighteenth century art, probably by the Bouchers and Fragonards which belonged to Paul Rosenberg, his dealer and neighbor. Certainly *The Siesta* (Museum of Modern Art, New York) 1919, one of the earliest and finest of Picasso's "colossal" groups, is close in composition and mood to Fragonard's *Scène Champêtre* (Collection Elie de Rothschild, Paris).

Picasso's first essays in the classical idiom tend to be as elegant as the design on a Greek mirror-back (e.g., No.), but in 1919 they become much more robust, so much so that the figures in them sometimes seem afflicted with a sort of elephantiasis. Specific parts of the body—legs, feet, arms and hands—are magnified with the result that women and occasionally men are metamorphosed into giants. "Disproportion of parts," as Fuseli said, "is the element of hugeness." However, after spending the summer at Dinard in 1922, Picasso returned to less voluminous forms; and some of his last essays in the classical style err once more in the direction of prettiness and refinement.

1

1. *Bathers*. Biarritz, 1918. Pencil, 9¹/₈ × 12¹/₄″. Fogg Art Museum, Cambridge, Mass. (Paul J. Sachs Collection).

2. *Woman with Pitcher (after a photograph)*. Paris, 1919. Pencil, 25⁷/₈ × 19³/₈″. Santa Barbara Museum of Art (Gift of Mr. Wright S. Ludington).

2

3

5

3. *Head of a Boy*. Paris, 1915. Oil on panel, 10¹/₂ × 7¹
   Mrs. Bertram Smith, New York.

4. *Apple*. Paris, 1918. Oil on canvas, 8¹/₂ × 10¹
   Private collection, New York.

5. *Interior*. Paris, 1919. Oil on canvas, 13¹/₄ × 9¹
   Mrs. John Jay Ide, New York.
   A corner of the studio in the apartment at 23 rue
   la Boétie, which Picasso had bought for himself
   his first wife, Olga, at the end of 1918. In the b.
   ground is the dome of Saint Augustin.

6

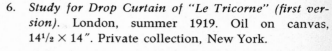

7

6. *Study for Drop Curtain of "Le Tricorne" (first version)*. London, summer 1919. Oil on canvas, 14¹/₂ × 14". Private collection, New York.

7. *Study for Drop Curtain of "Le Tricorne" (second version)*. London, summer 1919. Oil on canvas, 14³/₄ × 18". Private collection, New York.

8. *The Theater Box*. Paris, 1921. Oil on canvas, 75 × 57". Thannhauser Foundation, New York.
This section of the drop curtain which Picasso designed for the ballet, *"Cuadro Flamenco,"* was painted by the artist himself. It was intended as an ironical comment on Renoir's *"La Loge."*

8

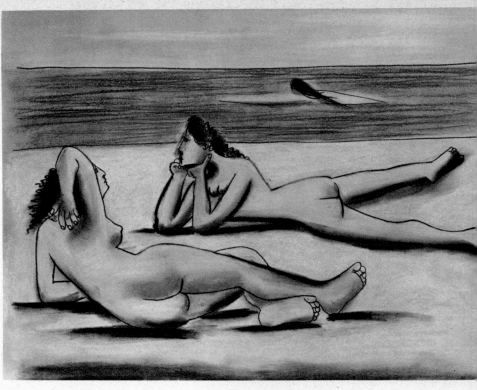

9. *Women at the Beach*. Juan-les-Pins, June 1920. Pastel, 20½ × 26″. Mr. and Mrs. Joseph H. Hazen, New York.

10. *Two Women*. Paris, 28 April 1920. Pastel and pencil, 25¾ × 19″. Private collection, New York.

11. *Standing Nude*. 1921. Oil on canvas, 10½ × Private collection, New York.

10   11

12.   *Three Bathers*. Juan-les-Pins, 19 August 1920. Pastel,
19¹/₄ × 25¹/₄″. Thannhauser Foundation, New York.

Satyr and Centaur. Juan-les-Pins, 12 September
1920. Watercolor, 9 × 11¹/₂″. Private collection,
New York.

14.   *Four Bathers*. 1921. Tempera on panel, 4 × 6″.
Private collection, New York.

15

16

Maternity. 1921. Oil on canvas, 25³/₄ × 18¹/₄".
Mr. and Mrs. Harry N. Abrams, New York.

Mother and Child. 1921. Oil on canvas, 40¹/₂ × 32".
Mr. and Mrs. Josef Rosensaft, New York.

Mother and Child. 1921. Oil on canvas, 38¹/₄ × 28".
Hillman Periodicals, Inc., New York.

Woman and Child. 1921. Oil on canvas, 56¹/₂ × 64".
The Art Institute of Chicago (Gift of Mary & Leigh
Block Charitable Fund, Inc., Mr. & Mrs. Edwin E.
Hokin, Maymar Corporation, Mr. & Mrs. Chauncey
McCormick, Mrs. Maurice L. Rothschild and the
Ada Turnbull Hertle Fund).

17

18

19

21

22

23

Head of a Man. 1921. Pastel, 24¹/₂ × 18″. Mr. and
Mrs. George Friedland, Merion, Pa.

Head of a Woman. 1921. Pastel, 25¹/₂ × 19⁵/₈″. Milwaukee Art Center (War Memorial Collection).

Head of a Woman. Dinard, 1922. Oil on canvas,
39 × 31¹/₂″. Cincinnati Art Museum.

Head of a Woman. 1921. Sanguine, 24¹/₄ × 18¹/₄″.
Mr. and Mrs. Allan Emil, New York.

Head of a Youth. Paris, 1922. Charcoal and pastel,
24 × 19″. Mr. and Mrs. Joseph Weinstein, New
York.

24

26

24. *La Toilette*. Dinard, 1922. Oil on canvas, 8³/₄ × 6
    Mr. Paul Hyde Bonner, Summerville, S.C.

25. *The Bather*. Dinard, 1922. Oil on panel, 7³/₈ ×
    The Wadsworth Atheneum, Hartford, Conn.
    Ella Gallup Sumner and Mary Catlin Su
    Collection).

26. *Woman in White Robe*. Paris, December
    Gouache on cardboard, 8¹/₄ × 6³/₄″. Allen Mem
    Art Museum, Oberlin College.

27. *Nude Woman Drying Her Feet*. 1921. P.
    26 × 20″. Private collection, New York.

28. *Woman with Blue Veil*. Paris, 1923. Oil on can
39½ × 32″. Los Angeles County Museum (Mr.
Mrs. George Gard De Sylva Collection).

29

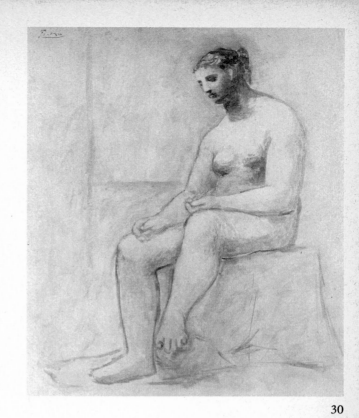

30

Woman by the Sea. Dinard, 1922. Oil on canvas, 23³/₄ × 19³/₄″. The Minneapolis Institute of Arts.

Seated Nude. Dinard, 1922. Oil on canvas, 25 × 21″. Dr. Herschel Carey Walker, New York.

Seated Woman. 1922. Oil on canvas, 37 × 27″. Thannhauser Foundation, New York.

31

32

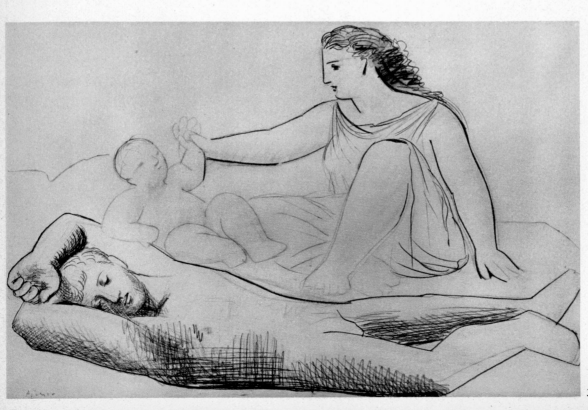

34

Mother and Child. Dinard, 1922. Oil on canvas, 39½ × 31½″. The Hon. and Mrs. W. Averell Harriman, New York.

Mother and Child. Dinard, 1922. Oil on canvas, 39½ × 31½″. The Baltimore Museum of Art (The Cone Collection).

The Family. Paris, 1923. Sanguine and oil on paper, 27¾ × 41¾″. Thannhauser Foundation, New York.

The Answer. 1923. Oil on canvas, 39¾ × 32¼″. Mrs. Cecil Blaffer Hudson, Houston.

The Sigh. 1923. Oil and charcoal on canvas, 23¾ × 19¾″. Mr. and Mrs. James Thrall Soby, New Canaan, Conn.
This picture was given this title by Jean Cocteau, who told Picasso that it looked as if it were "painted in sighs."

35

36

37. *Three Classical Figures*. Paris, 1923–24. Sang...
42 × 28¹/₄″. Mr. and Mrs. Hugh Chisholm,
York.

38. *The Pipes of Pan*. 1923. Pastel, 8³/₄ × 7⁷/₈″. Mr.
Mrs. Walter W. Weismann, New York.
According to Picasso, this is one of a serie...
studies for the large painting, *"The Pipes of ...
(Collection Picasso), which the artist regards a...
best work of the period. In the painting there...
only two figures, one of them in the same po...
the right-hand figure here.

38

PERLS GALLERIES

The Thirties

In 1931 Picasso bought the Château de Boisgeloup, on the borders of Normandy, as a refuge from the complications of Paris life. He converted the stables into sculpture studios and proceeded (1931–2) to execute a series of huge plaster figures and heads. A number of large paintings (Nos. 2–4) of the same time evoke the pneumatic charms of his new companion, Marie-Thérèse Walter. The exact opposite of Picasso's wife, Olga, Marie-Thérèse was an amiable, somewhat placid blonde addicted to sleeping and swimming: hence the many paintings of her in repose or bathing. She and her sister also inspired a number of compositions of two girls reading, writing and painting (No. 7). Many of the more important works of 1930–32 were painted with a view to their being included in the big 1932 exhibition at the Galerie Georges Petit, Paris (later in Zurich) —Picasso's first full-scale retrospective and a turning point in the public appreciation of his art.

As in the twenties, Picasso continued to visit the Mediterranean coast, usually Cannes or Juan-les-Pins, for several months every summer, and while there would execute numerous drawings and paintings with marine or classical themes. At the end of the season he would load his car with his work and return to Paris; one summer, however, the artist's car was robbed—these works have never been recovered. Picasso also returned to Spain in 1933 and 1934, which explains the resurgence of tauromachic themes at this time (No. 9). In the same period the influence of Surrealism manifests itself "for the first and last time" (Picasso insists), notably in a series of drawings (summer 1933) of *"personnages,"* constructed of heterogeneous objects, confronting one another on a beach. Besides revealing the influence of Lautréamont and André Breton, these disquieting works reflect the artist's despair at the collapse of his domestic life. An eighteen-month period (1935–36) of artistic inactivity is often said to have been a major consequence of these marital worries, but in fact Picasso continued to work, except when he indulged his usual habit of resting for a month or two, "in order to recharge my batteries." The only new development was that Picasso took to writing poetry: vivid strings of visual images in the manner of the Surrealists, but unmistakably Picassian.

In 1936 new conflicts made themselves felt. Marie-Thérèse had just given birth to the artist's daughter (Maïa), when Picasso, who had been vainly seeking a divorce from his wife, met and fell in love with Dora Maar (Nos. 19, 20 and 22). The progress of this romance can be followed in certain pictures of the period in which Picasso involuntarily wrenches the features of Marie-Thérèse into a likeness of his new friend. "How terrible," Picasso once admitted, "for a girl to see in my pictures that she is being supplanted." Marie-Thérèse and her daughter continue to figure in certain paintings, but Dora Maar's starry eyes and steadfast look dominate Picasso's work. In the last year of the thirties the artist comes to see anybody else he paints—Nusch Eluard (wife of the poet) or his Spanish maid, Inez—in terms of Dora; and he gradually accommodates his style to her personality—the personality that he had brought out in her. Even the women's heads in *Guernica* (1937)—Picasso's culminant achievement of the thirties, if not of his whole *œuvre*—have a general resemblance to Dora Maar, as witness No. 13, one of the studies for it. So vast was *Guernica* that Picasso was obliged to rent a special new studio, the second floor of a seventeenth century house on the rue des Grands-Augustins which is still his Paris headquarters. He also rented from the dealer, Ambroise Vollard, a house in the village of Le-Tremblay-sur-Mauldre, near Paris, where he spent several days a week hiding away from domestic worries and public attention.

During the last years of the thirties, Picasso's art became more agonized and shrill as the international situation deteriorated. Apart from *Guernica,* there are no overt references in his work to the threat of war. But the increasingly tortured heads of Dora Maar, the almost maniacal expressions of *The Girl with a Cock* (No. 16) and *The Man with a Lollipop* (No. 17) and the predatory look on the face of the bird-eating cat of the same date evoke an atmosphere of hysteria and sadism that was all too soon to become reality. When war broke out in 1939 Picasso was staying at Antibes, where he had been painting his large canvas, *The Night Fishers* (Museum of Modern Art, New York). He immediately left for Paris, but after three days realized that he would be better off in the provinces. He and Dora Maar accordingly installed themselves at Royan, a small port near Bordeaux, where Picasso worked intensively until, a year later, France fell.

1

2

1. *Pitcher and Bowl of Fruit*. Paris, 22 February 1931. Oil on canvas, 51½ × 64″. Private collection, New York.

2. *Woman in Armchair ("The Dream")*. Paris, 24 January 1932. Oil on canvas, 51 × 38″. Mr. and Mrs. Victor W. Ganz, New York.

3

3. *Bather Playing Ball*. Boisgeloup, 30 August 1932. Oil on canvas, 57$^{1}/_{2}$ × 45″. Private collection, New York.

4. *Reclining Nude*. Boisgeloup, July 1932. Oil on canvas, 40 × 36$^{1}/_{2}$″. Mr. and Mrs. Peter A. Rübel, New York.

4

5

5. *The Flower-Seller ("La Niçeuse")*. Mougins, summer
1937. Oil on canvas, 31⅞ × 25½″. Perls Galleries,
New York.
Although he almost never gives titles to his pictures,
Picasso inscribed "La Niçeuse" on the stretcher of
this painting. When told of his solecism—he should
have written "La Niçoise" (a woman of Nice)—the
artist replied, "It only goes to show I am still a
Spaniard."

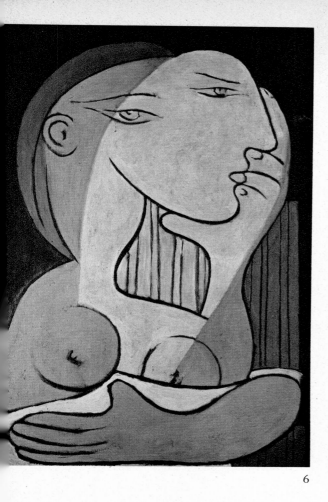

6

7

Seated Woman. Boisgeloup, summer 1932. Oil on panel, 29¼ × 20⅝". Mr. and Mrs. Lee A. Ault, New York.

Two Girls Reading. Boisgeloup, 28 March 1934. Oil on canvas. 36½ × 28¾". Dr. Herschel Carey Walker, New York.

Circus (Acrobats). Paris, 5 February 1933. Oil on canvas, 12⅞ × 16". Perls Galleries, New York. Picasso painted this after an evening at the Cirque Medrano with Tériade, the publisher of *Verve*.

8

9. *Bullfight*. Boisgeloup, 22 July 1934. Oil on canvas,
38 × 51″. Private collection, New York.
This was painted after Picasso's return from a pro-
longed trip round Spain, during which he went to
numerous bull-fights.

10. *Vase of Flowers and Fruit Dish on Window-Sill*.
Boisgeloup, 7 April 1934, Oil on canvas, 32 × 39½″.
Dr. Herschel Carey Walker, New York.

11. *Woman in a Red Hat*. Boisgeloup, September 1934.
Oil on canvas, 64 × 51″. Private collection, New
York.

12. *Fruit Dish and Jug*. Paris, 29 January 1937. Oil on
canvas, 21¼ × 28¾″. Mrs. Albert D. Lasker, New
York.

11

12

13

13. *African Sculpture in front of Window.* P[aris]
19 April 1937. Oil on canvas, 28½ × 23½". Mr. [and]
Mrs. Leo Simon, New York.
The African sculpture in this painting did not e[xist]
outside of Picasso's imagination.

14. *Weeping Woman (Study for "Guernica").* P[aris]
26 June 1937. Oil on canvas, 21 × 17½". Los A[nge]-
les County Museum (Gift of Mr. and Mrs. Tho[mas]
Mitchell).

15. *Cock.* Paris, 29 March 1938. Pastel, 30½ × 22[?"].
Private collection, New York.

14

15

16. *Girl with a Cock*. Paris, 15 February 1938. Oil on
canvas, 57¼ × 47½″. Mrs. Meric Callery, New
York (Courtesy of the Baltimore Museum of Art).

17. *Man with a Lollipop*. Mougins, 20 August 1938. Oil on paper mounted on canvas, 26⁷/₈ × 18″. Mr. Edward A. Bragaline, New York.

18. *Bull's Head and Pitcher*. Paris, 15 January 1939. Oil on canvas, 32 × 39¹/₂″. Private collection, New York.

19. *Woman in a Garden*. Le Tremblay, 10 December 1938. Oil on canvas, 51 × 38″. Mrs. Meric Callery, New York.

19

20

20. *Woman on Couch*. Paris, 21 January 1939. Oil on canvas, 38¼ × 51″. Private collection, New York. This work is a portrayal of Dora Maar. On the same day Picasso did a painting (Zervos, Vol. 9, No. 253) of his other companion, Marie–Thérèse Walter, in the same pose and setting.

21. *Nude Seated in Armchair*. Royan, 18 October 1939. Oil on canvas, 18¼ × 13″. Dr. Paul D. Wurzburger, Cleveland.

22. *Dora Maar*. Royan, 30 November 1939. Oil on canvas, 22 × 18″. Mr. and Mrs. Leon A. Mnuchin, New York.

21

22

STAEMPFLI GALLERY, Inc.

The Forties

Picasso spent the first year of the war at Royan, a port near Bordeaux. Because materials were in short supply, he was often forced to use ink and gouache instead of paint. Of the canvases that he painted during this period the anguished *Woman Dressing her Hair* (No. 1) is the most significant and gives the fullest expression to Picasso's wartime anxieties. In August 1940, shortly after the fall of France, the artist returned to Paris and spent the rest of the war either in his rue de la Boétie apartment, or rue des Grands-Augustins studio. A few blocks away lived Dora Maar whom Picasso saw every day; and down the street was the *Catalan* restaurant where he took his meals. For four years he seldom moved outside the area bounded by these points. The Germans left Picasso in peace, but the gloom and restricted pattern of his life is inevitably mirrored in his work, for instance in the bare lines that mark out the bleak, cell-like settings for still lifes and figure compositions (No. 2).

As Picasso admits, his paintings of the period were not conceived as war pictures (his only evocation of the war, *The Charnel House,* was painted after hostilities in Europe were over). Nevertheless, their wartime atmosphere makes itself felt at a subliminal level. Food, for instance, is painted nostalgically but in all its wartime meagerness, as in No. 4, where a drawerfull of agressive forks ("like souls in purgatory," says Picasso) are about to attack a length of sausage, two artichokes and the remains of a Camembert. In other still lifes Picasso makes a point of including a heatless radiator, symbol of wartime discomfort. Likewise, windows are blacked out, or shut, or they give onto gray skies. Skulls of men and beasts make disquieting appearances, notably in two *memento mori* still lifes painted when the artist heard that a Spanish friend had died. In general one cannot fail to notice the ugly angularity of everything, the austere and forceful way of painting, the colors that are somber and resonant or harshly strident, and the absence of all lyricism and sensuousness.

No less redolent of suffering is Picasso's most impressive achievement of the war and immediate pre-war period: the series of portraits, several hundred in number, in which the head of Dora Maar is submitted to a succession of fantastic distortions. True, Dora Maar's features suggested some of these deformations, but we must not leave out of account the anthropomorphic tendency in Picasso's work. Deliberately—and to some extent maliciously, because of latent animosity—the artist grafted the floppy ears and elongated muzzle of his Afghan dog, Kasbek, onto the face of Dora Maar. These "portraits" should also be seen as a deliberate attempt on the part of the artist to formulate a new canon of beauty in terms of what most people would call ugliness. That is why a dog-faced head of Dora, as in No. 1, is often a more powerful and convincing likeness—physiognomically as well as psychologically—than a more

conventional portrait like No. 5. As peace drew near, t spirit of Picasso's art lightened, but the portraits of Do Maar grew more and more virulent—a sign that the end her relationship with the artist was at hand.

During the liberation of Paris, Picasso amused hi self by doing a free version of Poussin's *Bacchanale*. Th was a prophetic work, for it pointed the way to the classic subject matter and mannerisms of the *Antipolis* series decorative paintings done for the Château Grimaldi Antibes in 1945—46. Once again Picasso reconciled own forward-looking style with backward glances at t distant past. Once again a change of circumstances sulted in a change of style. The end of the war, the beg ning of an idyllic new relationship (with Françoise Gil and the resumption of Mediterranean visits after an inter of five years are all reflected in these light-hearted *pastora* (Nos. 15 and 16) in which centaurs, satyrs and nym frolic and make love. Gone is the agonized look of Do Maar; instead Françoise serenely gazes out at us from series of radiant portraits (No. 13) often painted in a m ner that recalls Matisse.

From 1945 onward Picasso applied himself to lit graphy, completely revolutionizing the medium. He a injected new life into the art of ceramics, installing hims at Vallauris in order to do so. There, in 1948, Pica bought a derelict scent factory so as to have suffici studio space, and settled himself. Françoise and their t young children, Claude (born in 1947) and Paloma (born 1949), in a villa nearby. The decade ends with a spate paintings and lithographs, mainly of family life, wh testify to the artist's happiness.

1. *Nude Dressing her Hair*. Royan, 6 March 1940. Oil on canvas, 51¼ × 38⅛″. Mrs. Bertram Smith, New York.

2. *Reclining Nude.* Paris, 30 September 1942. Oil on canvas, 51¼ × 76¾″. Private collection, New York.

3

3. *Still Life with Oranges*. Paris, 10 June 1941. Oil on canvas, 28 × 35¹/₂″. Mr. and Mrs. Fernand Leval, New York.

4. *Still Life with Sausage*. Paris, 10 May 1041. Oil on canvas, 35 × 25¹/₂″. Mr. and Mrs. Victor W. Ganz, New York.

5. *Portrait of Dora Maar.* Paris, 9 October 1942. Oil on pand, 36¼ × 28¾". Private collection, New York.

6. *The Striped Bodice.* Paris, 20 September 1943. Oil on canvas, 40 × 32½". Private collection, New York.

7. *Woman in Green.* Paris, 1943. Oil on canvas, 51 × 38". Mr. and Mrs. James Johnson Sweeney, New York.

5

6

8. *The Caged Owl*. Paris, 24 March 1947. Oil on canv
28¹/₂ × 35¹/₂″. Staempfli Gallery, Inc., New York.

9. *Tomato Plant*. Paris, 10 August 1944. Oil on canv
36 × 28″. Mr. and Mrs. Vladimir Golschmann, N
York.

10. *Tomato Plant and Carafe*. Paris, 3 August 1944. C
on canvas, 28³/₄ × 36¹/₄″. Mr. Edgar M. Bronfma
New York.

9

10

11. *The Sailor*. Paris, 28 October 1943. Oil on canvas, 51½ × 35½". Private collection, New York.

12

Seated Woman and Standing Nude in Interior. Paris,
April 1944. Oil on canvas, 28 × 36″. Mr. and Mrs.
Morton G. Neumann, Chicago.

Ile de la Cité, Paris. Paris, 26 February 1945. Oil on
canvas, 31 × 48″. Mrs. Albert D. Lasker, New York.

13

14

15

16

17. *Cock and Knife*. Paris, 21 March 1947. Oil on canvas, 31⅞ × 39⅜". Private collection, New York.

18. *The Owl*. Paris, 1 January 1947 (repainted later the same year). Oil on canvas, 48⅝ × 41". Perls Galleries, New York.

CORDIER-WARREN GALLERY

The Fifties

The 1950's correspond roughly to Picasso's seventies, an age at which one might expect a certain deceleration. Picasso, characteristically, increased his pace and produced more paintings and branched out in more directions than most artists in a lifetime. At the beginning of the decade he was living with Françoise Gilot (No. 1) and their two children in an ugly little villa, *La Galloise,* at Vallauris. Numerous paintings of the family separately (No. 2) and together, and sometimes playing with Picasso's boxer dog, Jan, reflect the artist's contentment. This did not last. The outbreak of war in Korea deeply distressed Picasso, as witness the two huge, polemical panels, *War* and *Peace* (1952). At the same time his relationship with Françoise deteriorated, and the couple parted in 1953. This gave rise to the drawings (the so-called *Verve* series), done at the end of 1953 and the beginning of 1954, which comment ironically on the plight of an elderly artist involved with a younger woman.

During the first half of 1954 Picasso's morale was low. In the absence of female companionship, he traveled restlessly around the south of France visiting friends and going to bullfights. Toward the end of this bleak period Picasso painted some fifteen tender portraits of Sylvette David (No. 3) which have had wide appeal, anticipating the fashion for the kind of looks that Brigitte Bardot has popularized. In the final portraits of Sylvette the features subtly change their cast; this is because the artist had fallen in love with the young and beautiful Jacqueline Roque and, as always, had begun to see other people in terms of his beloved. A number of portraits (No. 4) done in a new style in keeping with the looks and appearance of his sitter, reflect the artist's new-found happiness. Later in the year, when he went to Paris, Picasso took Jacqueline with him, and while there he painted an impressive series of variations on Delacroix's *Femmes d'Alger* (Nos. 6—18)—oblique allusions to the Delacroix-like looks of his companion.

Soon after Picasso returned to the Mediterranean (early in 1955), he installed himself in *La Californie,* a vast Edwardian villa at Cannes. Here he continued to draw and paint Jacqueline, occasionally from life but more often from memory, and frequently in Algerian costume (No. 21). He also devoted most of the summer to the film that he made with Georges-Henri Clouzot, *Le Mystère Picasso,* which reveals to the public his methods of working. The only blemish on Picasso's happiness was Jacqueline's health, which remained a source of worry for the next two or three years; hence the numerous portraits in which her features are twisted into a grimace of suffering. All the same, Picasso continued to work with astonishing brilliance and prolificacy at ceramics, sculpture and lithographs as well as painting. In a spirit of proprietary pride he painted some thirty-five pictures of his studio (Nos. 20 and 24) in which once again there is a hint of orientalism. Halfway through the series a small figure of Jacqueline is introduced into the composition; gradually she comes to dominate and the studio dwindles to nothing. Other favorite subje of the period include the artists children, usually paint during their summer and Christmas holiday visits, a bullfight scenes (No. 25), usually painted on Sundays, wh Picasso regrets not being present at an actual *corrida.*

In August 1957, Picasso shut himself away from t world and did not re-emerge until he had executed fourte decorative paintings of pigeons nesting on his studio b cony, and forty-four free variations on Velasquez' I *Meninas:* "a battle to the death" (Picasso's words) with t Spanish master. At one moment the artist contemplat involving El Greco and Goya in the fray in order to arri at a quintessential Spanish painting, but he ultimately l the series (which he has presented to the city of Barcelor as a testimonial to his passionate, if mixed, feelings Velasquez' *chef d'œuvre.* In the following year (19 Picasso once again reverted to Velasquez in *The Urchin Vauvenargues,* a pastiche in the manner of *Los Borrach* This was one of the first pictures to be painted at t Château de Vauvenargues, near Aix-en-Provence, wh he had recently purchased and which inspired him to pa in a somewhat Spanish manner. In the last three ye Spanish themes have recurred in Velasquez-like drawir of Jacqueline on horseback, and innumerable tauromac scenes. But the most significant of Picasso's recent achie ments—over a hundred drawings and paintings af Manet's *Déjeuner sur l'Herbe*—have nothing to do w Spain. In these Picasso arrives at a synthesis of French of the past and present. Not only Manet, but Pouss Cézanne and the Impressionists are made to lose th separate identities and become one with Picasso.

Shortly before Picasso's eightieth birthday (Octol 1961), the construction of a skyscraper next door to *Californie* forced him to move away, and he is now instal in a large villa in the country near Mougins. Here, seclusion, he has been painting his favorite subject, J queline, whom he recently married. Once again his st has changed, and he sees her partly in terms of Manet a partly in terms of his Afghan dog, Kabul. But these "d faced" portraits are painted with affection and hum qualities that recur in much of his recent work. From evidence of his recent activities alone, the present wo seem to be the most serene and contented period of Pic so's life.

Seated Nude. Vallauris, 1953. Oil on canvas, $51^{1/4} \times 37^{3/4}$". City Art Museum of St. Louis (Gift of Mr. and Mrs. Joseph Pulitzer, Jr.).

Paloma Asleep. Vallauris, 28 December 1952. Oil on panel, $44^{7/8} \times 57^{1/2}$". Mrs. Bertram Smith, New York.

Paloma is Picasso's youngest child (born 1949) by Françoise Gilot.

1

2

3

4

3. *Portrait of Sylvette David*. Vallauris, 5 May 1
   Oil on canvas, 33 × 26″. Dr. Herschel Carey Wa
   New York.
   Sylvette David, daughter of a Parisian art-de
   was the model for some fifteen portraits which
   casso painted in spring 1954.

4. *Portrait of Jacqueline*. Cannes, June 1954. Oi
   canvas, 36¼ × 28¾″. Mr. and Mrs. Allan D. I
   New York.
   One of the first portraits that Picasso painted of
   queline Roque who subsequently became his se
   wife.

5

5. *Winter Landscape*. Vallauris, 22 December 1950.
Oil on panel, 40½ × 49½″. Mr. and Mrs. Victor
W. Ganz, New York.

6. *The Women of Algiers, after Delacroix. A.* Paris,
   13 December 1954, Oil on canvas, 23⁵/₈ × 28³/₄″.
   Dr. Herschel Carey Walker, New York.
   This and the next twelve paintings comprise all but
   two of Picasso's fifteen variations on Delacroix's
   "Les Femmes d'Alger" (Louvre). The choice of
   subject was largely prompted by the resemblance
   between the girl with the hookah in the Delacroix
   and Jacqueline Roque whom the artist had met nine
   months earlier. Picasso had not seen the Delacroix

original for some years, and, when working on
series, banished all reproductions of it from
studio, lest it "hamper his imagination."

7. *The Women of Algiers, after Delacroix. B.* Pa
   13 December 1954. Oil on canvas, 23⁵/₈ × 28³
   Mr. and Mrs. Wilbur D. May, Reno.

8. *The Women of Algiers, after Delacroix. C.* Pa
   28 December 1954. Oil on canvas, 21¹/₄ × 25⁵
   Private collection, New York.

7

8

9

11

The Women of Algiers, after Delacroix. D. Paris, 1 January 1955. Oil on canvas, $18\frac{1}{8} \times 21\frac{5}{8}''$. Paul Rosenberg and Co., New York.

The Women of Algiers, after Delacroix. E. Paris, 16 January 1955. Oil on canvas, $18\frac{1}{8} \times 21\frac{5}{8}''$. Mr. and Mrs. Wilbur D. May, Reno.

The Women of Algiers, after Delacroix. F. Paris, 17 January 1955. Oil on canvas, $21\frac{1}{4} \times 25\frac{5}{8}''$. Mr. and Mrs. Lawrence D. Saidenberg, New York.

The Women of Algiers, after Delacroix. H. Paris, 24 January 1955. Oil on canvas, $51\frac{1}{8} \times 63\frac{3}{4}''$. Private collection, New York.

12

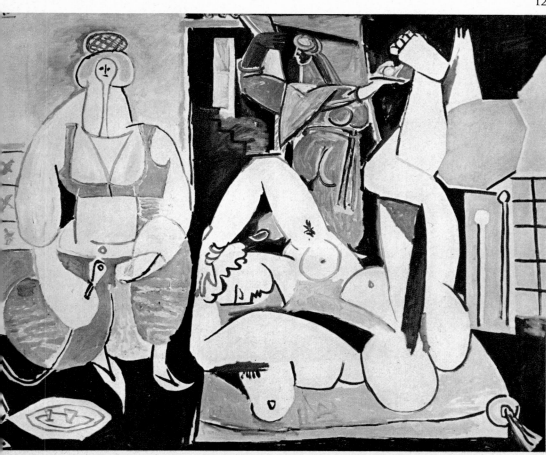

13

14

43. *The Women of Algiers, after Delacroix. J.* Paris,
26 January 1955. Oil on canvas, 44⅞ × 57½".
Paul Rosenberg and Co., New York.

44. *The Women of Algiers, after Delacroix. K.* Paris,
6 February 1955. Oil on canvas, 51⅛ × 63¾".
Private collection, New York.

45. *The Women of Algiers, after Delacroix. L.* Paris,
9 February 1955. Oil on canvas, 51¼ × 38⅛".
Paul Rosenberg and Co., New York.

46. *The Women of Algiers, after Delacroix. M.* Paris,
11 February 1955. Oil on canvas, 51¼ × 76¾".
Private collection, New York.

15

16

17

18

7. *The Women of Algiers, after Delacroix.* N. Paris,
    13 February 1955. Oil on canvas, 44⅞ × 57½".
    Washington University, St. Louis (Gift of Mrs. Etta
    Steinberg).

8. *The Women of Algiers, after Delacroix.* O. Paris,
    14 February 1955. Oil on canvas, 44⅞ × 57½".
    Mr. and Mrs. Victor W. Ganz, New York.

9. *Faun by Starlight.* Cannes, July 1955. Oil on can-
    vas, 36½ × 29". Mr. and Mrs. Joseph H. Hazen,
    New York.

10. *The Studio.* Cannes, 24 October 1955. Oil on can-
    vas, 75¾ × 29¾". Saidenberg Gallery, New York.
    This and No. 24 depict the studio at *"La Cali-
    fornie,"* the large villa at Cannes where Picasso
    lived from 1954 until 1961, and which he still
    owns.

20

19

21

22

21. *Woman in Turkish Costume*. Cannes, 26 November 1955. Oil on canvas, 45³/₄ × 35″. Perls Galleries, New York.

22. *Seated Nude*. Cannes, 3 January 1956. Oil on canvas, 45³/₄ × 35″. Mr. and Mrs. Saidenberg, New York.

23. *Jardinière with Ferns*. Cannes, 5 June 1956. Oil on canvas, 63³/₄ × 51¹/₈″. Private collection, New York. This represents the remains of a silver-painted basket on a stand, tied with a mauve bow and filled with ferns and flowers, which the artist received as a birthday gift. Its interesting "armature," no less than its banality, intrigued the artist so much that he ultimately painted this picture of it. "I wanted to do a Manet," he said.

24. *The Studio*. Cannes, 1 April 1956. Oil on canvas, 35 × 45³/₄″. Private collection, New York.

23

24

25

25. *Bullfight*. Cannes, 19 May 1956. Oil on canvas,
    19⅝ × 24″. Mr. and Mrs. Saidenberg, New York.

26. *The Breakfast*. Cannes, 19 April 1960. Oil on can-
    vas, 28¾ × 36¼″. Saidenberg Gallery, New York.

27. *Seated Woman in a Blue Armchair*. Cannes, 23 April
    1960. Oil on canvas, 39½ × 32″. Saidenberg Gallery,
    New York.

26

THE NEW GALLERY

Drawings

Since Picasso is probably the most prolific and eclectic and, in the opinion of many, the most gifted draughtsman in the history of art, it is impossible to do full justice to his drawings in a single exhibition. The fifty sheets assembled here should, however, chart the course of his graphic development.

"I drew long before I could speak," Picasso recalls, "but I never drew like a child." This is borne out by his earliest surviving drawings, done at the age of seven, of clumsy, but properly proportioned figures and perspectively accurate scenes. By the age of eleven he was producing academic studies of which the most accomplished art student could be proud. While still in his teens, his prowess as a draughtsman was such that his art-teacher father made over his palette to him; and instead of taking a month to pass the entrance examination into the Barcelona Academy of Fine Arts, when he was sixteen, he sailed through in a day. Small wonder that the established local artists watched his triumphant progress with amazement tinged with rancor. "You have no idea how easily things come to me," Picasso once said. "This is what I have always had to fight. I have had to make things difficult for myself."

Picasso was a great draughtsman before he was a great painter. Until he was twenty-five he spent much of his time filling sketchbooks with vivid, accurate observations of everyday life. Some of these drawings are highly finished, but even the merest sketches of relations or friends, street scenes or café life have an astonishing immediacy and humanity as well as technical virtuosity. Perhaps Picasso was already trying to live up to Delacroix's advice to a student, a *mot* that he likes to quote: "If you have not sufficient skill to make a sketch of a man throwing himself out of a window, in the time that it takes him to fall from the fourth floor to the ground, you will never be capable of producing great *machines*."

Picasso's use of pen or pencil has not always been a question of preference. Until 1905 paint and canvas were luxuries that he often had to deny himself; hence many blue and pink period pictures are painted in gouache on cardboard. Again, in 1914–18 and in 1939–44, wartime shortages occasionally obliged Picasso to work on paper rather than canvas. Most of his life, however, Picasso has been in a position to do exactly what he likes, to draw on newspaper or on sheets of eighteenth century paper, as he chooses, and in any medium or style that pleases him. Alternately bold or meticulous, academic or iconoclastic, caricatural or classical, Ingresque or Rembrandtian in approach, Picasso can suit his style to his subject, his medium, his surroundings or his whim. In the same sketchbook realistic bullfights alternate with schematic nudes, idyllic portraits of a current favorite with scenes of Rabelaisian farce.

It is no good looking for a consistent pattern in Picas-so's approach to draughtsmanship. Sometimes we find [a] mass of drawings done for a specific picture, sometimes [a] whole series done *after* a picture, more often a picture [for] which no studies exist. Frequently drawings resembl[e] paintings of the same period; occasionally they do not lo[ok] as if they were by the same hand. Part of the explanati[on] is that Picasso seldom goes straight for a subject, but wo[rks] towards it circuitously from various angles, depending [on] the vagaries of his extraordinary imagination. But even [if] Picasso did work in a predictable way, it would still [be] impossible to isolate his drawings from the rest of [his] *œuvre*, because drawing plays a dominant part in all [his] artistic activities. Indeed, many of Picasso's paintings [of] the last forty years—even the monumental *Guernica*—[are] either conceived in graphic terms or are drawings execut[ed] in paint. Conversely, many of Picasso's so-called drawi[ngs] belong by rights to the realm of painting.

Drawing has always been one of the necessities [of] Picasso's life. If pen, pencil or paper is not available, [he] has been known to make do with lipstick on a girl's l[ips], pieces of chalk on a friend's automobile, a red-hot po[ker] on the vellum cover of a book, and match sticks, cigare[tte] ends, coffee and even the sap of a flower on a paper ta[ble]cloth. The very impermanence and freakishness of th[ese] improvised media appeal to Picasso's humor; and [he] recalls with delight his project—never, alas, accomplish[ed] —of tatooing Braque's body with cubist drawings [of] guitars, newspapers and fruit dishes. No matter h[ow] ephemeral or frivolous, these *jeux d'esprit* have validity [by] virtue of being Picassos. For Picasso is one of the very f[ew] artists of whom it can be said that everything by him, fr[om] the merest scrawl to the most elaborate drawing, bears [in] some degree the mark of his genius, because everyth[ing] that he does, even adressing a letter, is done with to[tal] concentration. This is what the artist means, when he s[ays] half seriously, half jokingly: "There is no such thing a[s a] bad Picasso; some are less good than others."

1

Cocks. Barcelona, 1896. Conté crayon, 10¹/₄ × 16¹/₂″.
Private collection, New York.

Self Portrait. Barcelona, 1899. Charcoal, 18¹/₄ × 21″.
Dr. Herschel Carey Walker, New York.

2

3

Picasso

4

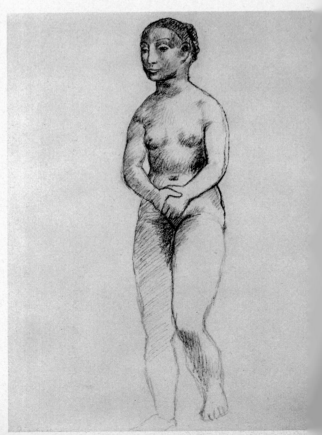

6

7

8

9

9. *African Head.* Paris, 1907. Conté crayon, 11⁷/₈ × 9³/₈″.
Mr. and Mrs. Georges E. Seligmann, New York.

10. *Standing Nude Woman.* Paris, 1907. Gouache,
24³/₄ × 18¹/₂″. Private collection, New York.

11. *Still Life with Glass.* Paris, 1909. Ink and watercolor,
9 × 13¹/₂″. Private collection, New York.

12. *Still Life with Fan.* Paris, 1909. Charcoal, 12¹/₈ × 18⁷/₈″.
Mrs. John D. Rockefeller 3rd, New York.

13. *Head of a Woman.* Paris, spring 1909. Ink and
watercolor, 24¹/₂ × 18¹/₂″. Mr. and Mrs. Walter Ross,
New York.

10

11

12

13

14

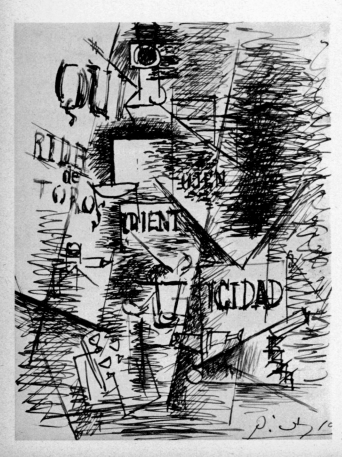

14. *Standing Nude*. Paris, spring 1910. Ink and wat
color, 12 × 4³/₄″. Private collection, New York.

15. *Standing Figure*. 1911–12. Ink, 12 × 7³/₄″. Mrs. B
tram Smith, New York.

16. *Still Life with Bullfight Poster, Bottle and F*
Spring, 1912. Ink, 6³/₄ × 5″. Private collection, N
York.

17. *Still Life ("La Negrita")*. Paris, 1914. Pen
14¹/₄ × 17³/₄″. Mr. and Mrs. Stephen Hahn, N
York.

18. *Man with a Pipe*. Paris, 1915. Pencil, 10³/₄ × 8¹/
Mr. and Mrs. Saidenberg, New York.

19. *Seated Harlequin*. Montrouge, 1918. Pencil a
conté crayon, 13 × 9¹/₂″. The New Gallery, N
York.

16

17

19

20

22

20. *Woman with Rosary*. Paris, 1919. Pencil, 12½ × 8½″. Private collection, New York.

21. *Portrait of Charpentier*. Paris, 1920. Pencil, 13¼ × 9¼″. Mr. Francis G. Guth, New York.

22. *Woman in Armchair*. Paris, November 1920. Charcoal, 10¼ × 8″. Private collection, New York.

23. *Three Bathers*. Fontainebleau, 14 May 1921. Watercolor and ink wash, 9¼ × 13¼″. The New Gallery, New York.

24. *Serenade*. Paris, 1923. Pen and ink wash, 9½ × 12½″. Mr. and Mrs. Daniel Saidenberg, New York.

23

24

25

26

25. *Standing Nude*. Paris, 1923. Ink wash, 24¼ × 18½″. Mr. and Mrs. James W. Alsdorf, Winnetka, Ill.

26. *Three Dancers at Rest*. Paris, 1925. Ink, 13¾ × 9¾″. Private collection, New York.

27. *Head of a Woman*. Paris, 1926. Charcoal and white chalk, 25 × 19″. Private collection, New York.

27

28

29

28. *Portrait of Man Ray*. Paris, 3 January 1934. Pen and ink wash, 13⅝ × 9¾″. Mr. and Mrs. Paul Kantor, Beverly Hills.

29. *Bull with Woman and Horse*. Boisgeloup, 16 April 1935. Charcoal, 13½ × 20″. Mr. and Mrs. Lee A. Ault, New York.

30

31

32

33

34

35

36

35. *Woman, Child and Cat in Interior*. Mougins,
    5 August 1938. Pen and ink wash, 17$^1/_2$ × 26$^5/_8$″.
    Private collection, New York.

36. *Standing Nude*. Mougins, 5 July 1938. Pen and ink
    wash, 8$^1/_4$ × 5$^1/_2$″. Mr. and Mrs. Lee A. Ault, New
    York.

37. *Man with Lollipop*. Mougins, 23 July 1938. Pencil,
12 × 9¹/₂″. Mr. and Mrs. Lee A. Ault, New York.

38

40

38. *Woman in a Tub*. Royan, 19 September 1
   Gouache, 25¹/₂ × 17¹/₂″. Mr. and Mrs. Saiden
   New York.

39. *Reclining Nude*. Paris, 25 January 1941. Gou
   on wood, 7 × 10¹/₄″. Mr. and Mrs. Nathan L.
   pern, New York.

40. *Ram's Skull and Grapes*. Royan, 1 October
   Ink wash, 18¹/₂ × 25¹/₂″. Mr. Alexander Liber
   New York.

41

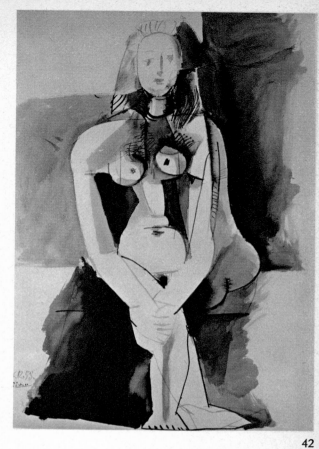

42

Nude. Paris, 28 November 1941. Ink, 15⁷/₈ × 11⁷/₈″.
The Solomon R. Guggenheim Museum, New York.

Seated Woman. Vallauris, 6 December 1953. Pen
and ink wash, 27¹/₂ × 19³/₄″. Mr. and Mrs. Paul
Kantor, Beverly Hills.

Battle of Centaurs. Golfe-Juan, August 1946. Pen
and ink wash, 20 × 26″. Private collection, New
York

43

44. *The Studio (Models Posing).* Vallauris, 11 January 1954. Ink wash, 9¹/₂ × 12⁵/₈″. Private collection, New York.

45. *The Studio (The Lady Painter).* Vallauris, 21 January 1954. Ink wash, 9¹/₂ × 12⁵/₈″. Private collection, New York.

46. *Bacchanale.* Cannes, 22 September 1955. Ink and crayon, 19¹/₂ × 25¹/₂″. Mr. and Mrs. Saidenberg, New York.

44

46

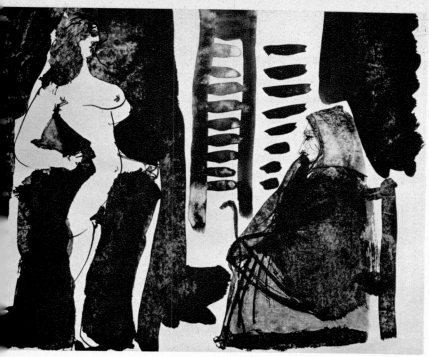

47

Young Girl and Duenna. Cannes, 17 June 1960.
Pen and ink wash, 13³/₄ × 17¹/₄″. Private collection,
New York.

Girl in Mantilla. Cannes, 10 June 1960. Pen and
ink wash, 21¹/₂ × 15″. Dr. Herschel Carey Walker,
New York.

48

49. *Girl before a Mirror*. Cannes, 9 September 1960. Scraperboard, 11⅞ × 9⅝″. Private collection, New York.

50. *Standing Nude Man*. Paris, 1907. Gouache, 24½ × 18½″. Madame Helena Rubinstein, New York.

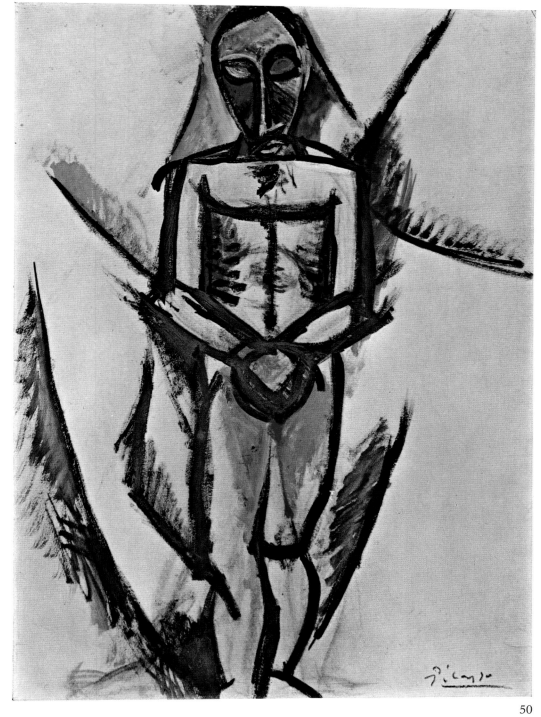

1

1. *Absinthe Glass*. Paris, 1914. Painted bronze and
    metal spoon, 8¹⁄₂″ high. The Museum of Modern
    Art, New York (Gift of Mrs. Bertram Smith).

OTTO GERSON GALLERY

Sculpture

Picasso's achievements as a painter overshadow the fact that he is also the most inventive sculptor of the twentieth century. Since some of his most important pieces have not been cast, let alone published or exhibited, a show drawn from private and public collections can give only a partial view of Picasso as a sculptor.

Picasso usually turns to sculpture as a reaction against painting, or when he needs help with pictorial problems. For instance, his earliest known sculpture (No. 2) is the first idea for a pose which recurs in numerous blue period paintings of a slightly later date. In 1906–07, when he was trying to evolve a new formal vocabulary, Picasso briefly resorted to sculpture (Nos. 9–11), this time deriving inspiration from archaic Iberian heads. Again, in 1909, at a crucial point in his cubist development, Picasso's investigations into the pictorial representation of form were furthered by a plaster that was later cast in bronze: the faceted *Head of a Woman* (No. 12). And the little *Glass of Absinthe* (No. 1) is a brilliant attempt to solve a pictorial problem in sculptural terms.

It is no coincidence that Picasso ceased to sculpt between 1913 and 1927, the span of the synthetic cubist period. For the problems that concerned the artist at this time were essentially anti-sculptural; their solution lay in respecting the two-dimensional surface of paper or canvas. Just as anti-sculptural, though in a different way, are the works of Picasso's classical phase, for all that they were inspired by Greek and Roman marbles and conceived in plastic terms. To have carried out these monumental compositions in the round would have taken even Picasso a lifetime, so he did paintings of them in what amounts to *trompe l'œil*. Here we must also take into account Picasso's tendency to be a sculptor *manqué* when he is painting, and *vice versa*—part of his campaign to destroy the frontiers between different artistic techniques.

The interaction between painting and sculpture is nowhere more evident than in the monumental figure paintings and drawings that Picasso did in 1927–28. "I have to paint them," Picasso said, "because nobody will commission one from me"—and small wonder, since they were conceived on the scale of a three-story house. Renewed contact with Gonzalez, inventor of welded metal sculpture, resulted in Picasso adopting various new techniques between 1928 and 1934. With Gonzalez' help he made open-work constructions of metal rods, which realize in three-dimensional form the delicate scaffolding of his paintings; and he welded heterogeneous metal objects, saucepan lids, springs and other *éléments réels* into hallucinatory heads and figures—prototypes for many of today's assemblages.

The conversion into workshops of part of the Château de Boisgeloup—the house he bought in 1931—provided Picasso with further encouragement to sculpt. Nor had he far to look for a suitable subject. His new companion, Marie-

Thérèse Walter, had a magnificently sculptural face and body, as witness the monumental heads and voluptuous nudes that she inspired between 1930 and 1934—works which Picasso has never released. Toward the end of this period of plastic activity, the artist summed up his conflicting feelings in a suite of engravings (1933)—classical both in theme and manner—which show an aging, but still virile sculptor at work in different styles and diverting himself in the company of his models.

After 1934, Picasso neglected sculpture until he returned to Paris in 1941. Some of his pieces done during the Occupation reveal Picasso's genius for improvisation when materials were in short supply—for example a bull's head made out of the handlebars and saddle of a bicycle and a bird made out of a child's scooter. Later (1943) he was able to lay hands on a supply of modeling clay which sufficed for small items like the *Cat* (No. 15) as well as for the heroic head of Dora Maar, and what is perhaps Picasso' most important sculpture, the archaically simple *Man with a Lamb* (No. 14).

In 1940, Picasso moved to Vallauris, largely because he wanted to work in ceramics—"sculpture without tears," he says, because it allows him to work quickly and easily in three dimensions and in color. He also embarked on a new phase of plastic inventiveness. Picasso's most important sculptures of the Vallauris period (1948–53) were usually executed in plaster combined with all kinds of miscellaneous objects and later cast in bronze. For example the head of *The Baboon and Young* (No. 2) is constructed out of two toy automobiles, the *Girl Reading a Book* (No. 24) out of a block of wood and some screws, and the *Crane* (No. 23) out of a fork and assorted hardware. Even more heterogeneous are two major, but as yet uncast pieces of this period, a life-size *Girl with Skipping-Rope* and *Woman Wheeling a Baby Carriage,* both of about 195. As in his work of the early thirties, the artist has managed to transform everyday objects into sculpture of startling immediacy. The same is also true of the recent *Bathers* (No. 32 A–F), which were pieced together out of bits of flotsam, bamboo and planks of wood, before being cast in bronze.

In his eightieth year (1960–61), Picasso tried yet another new approach to sculpture. Out of cut and folded paper he constructed a series of heads, birds and life-size figures (not to mention a chair) which he then had copied in sheet metal and painted. The result is a series of ingenious works which could almost serve as instruction models to demonstrate the basic principles of cubism. These and the rest of Picasso's sculpture have recently been moved to a new and as yet virgin studio in his house at Mougins, where the artist is preparing himself for another spell of sculptural activity.

2

3

4

2. *Seated Woman*. Barcelona, 1901. Bronze, 5¹/₂″ high.
    Dr. and Mrs. Peritz Levinson, New York.
    This bronze has hitherto been dated 1899. Picasso
    now says that he did no sculpture before 1900 and
    that this, probably his earliest attempt at modelling,
    was done at the same time as paintings of women
    in the same pose.

3. *Mask of Man with Broken Nose*. Paris 1904—05.
    Bronze, 7³/₄″ high. Otto Gerson Gallery, New York.

4. *Head of Alice Derain*. Paris 1905. Bronze, 10³/₄″
    high. Saidenberg Gallery, New York.

5

7

Head of a Jester. Paris 1905. Bronze, 16½" high. Mr. and Mrs. William B. Jaffe, New York.

Head of Fernande. Paris, late 1905. Bronze, 14" high. Otto Gerson Gallery, New York.

Kneeling Woman Combing her Hair. Paris, 1906. Bronze, 16½" high. The Baltimore Museum of Art (The Cone Collection).

Head of a Man. Paris, early 1906. Bronze, 7¾" high. The Baltimore Museum of Art (The Cone Collection).

Head of a Woman. Paris, late 1906. Bronze, 6⅛ × 4". Joseph H. Hirshhorn Collection, New York.

8

9

10

10. *Head of a Girl*. Paris, late 1906. Bronze, 4³/₄″ high
Mr. and Mrs. William Zeckendorf, Jr., New York.

11. *Head of a Woman*. Paris, 1907. Bronze, 7¹/₂″ high
Mr. and Mrs. Sampson R. Field, New York.

12. *Head of a Woman*. Paris, late 1909. Bronze, 16¹/₄
high. Joseph H. Hirshhorn Collection, New York.

13. *Decorated Cup*. Paris, 1921. Silver, 3³/₈″ high
Private collection, New York. (Not illustrated)

14. *Man with a Lamb*. Paris, 1944. Bronze, 87″ hig
Mr. and Mrs. R. Sturgis Ingersoll and the Phil
delphia Museum of Art.

11

12

14

15

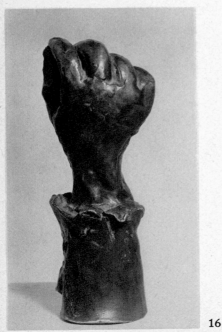

16

15. *Cat*. Paris, 1944. Bronze, 14½″ high. Mr. and M
    Richard K. Weil, St. Louis.

16. *Hand*. Paris, 1947. Bronze, 9½″ long. Mrs. H. G.
    Lloyd, Haverford, Pa.

17. *Angry Owl*. Vallauris, 1950. Bronze, 14″ h
    Mr. and Mrs. Morton G. Neumann, Chicago.

18. *Owl*. Vallauris, 1950. Bronze. 15½″ high. The
    Mr. Louis E. Stern, New York.

19. *Little Owl*. Vallauris, 1953. Painted bronze, 10
    high. Joseph H. Hirshhorn Collection, New Yo

20. *Little Owl*. Vallauris, 1953. Painted bronze, 1
    high. Private collection, New York.

17

18

19

20

21. *Baboon and Young*. Vallauris, 1951. Bronze, 21″
high. Private collection, New York.

2. *Jug and Figs*. Valauris, 1952. Painted bronze, 19″ long. Mr. and Mrs. Morton G. Neumann, Chicago.

3. *Crane*. Vallauris, 1952. Painted bronze, 29½″ high. Mr. and Mrs. George Staempfli, New York.

4. *Girl Reading a Book*. Vallauris, 1952—53. Painted bronze, 14″ long. Mr. and Mrs. Gerald Gidwitz, Highland Park, Ill.

22

23

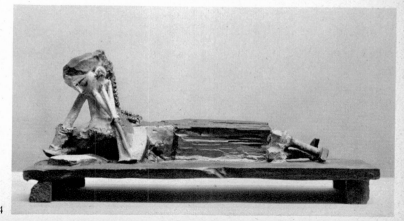

24

25

26

25. *Bouquet.* Vallauris, 1953. Bronze, 24″ high. Otto Gerson Gallery, New York.

26. *Flowers in a Vase.* Vallauris, 1953. Bronze, 24″ high. Mr. and Mrs. Harry L. Bradley, Milwaukee.

27. *Vase and Cake Dish.* Vallauris, 1953. Bronze, 33½″ high. Mr. and Mrs. Walter B. Ford, Grosse Point Farms, Mich.

28. *Woman's Head.* Cannes, 1957. Bronze, 14″ high. Mr. and Mrs. Joseph Weinstein, New York.

29. *Bull.* Cannes, 1958. Bronze, 4¾″ long. Private collection, New York.

30. *Bull.* Cannes, 1957. Bronze, 6½″ long. Mr. Larry Aldrich, New York.

31. *Bull's Head.* Cannes, 1957. Bronze, 5″ high. Mr. and Mrs. Saidenberg, New York.

27

29

30

28

31

32. *Six Bathers*. Cannes, 1956. Bronze. Otto Ge
    Gallery, New York.
    A. *Standing Man*. 104$^{1}/_{8}$″ high.
    B. *Man with Clasped Hands*. 84$^{1}/_{2}$″ high.
    C. *Standing Man*. 89$^{5}/_{8}$″ high.
    D. *Woman with Outstretched Arms*. 78″ high.
    E. *Boy*. 69″ high.
    F. *Child*. 53″ high.

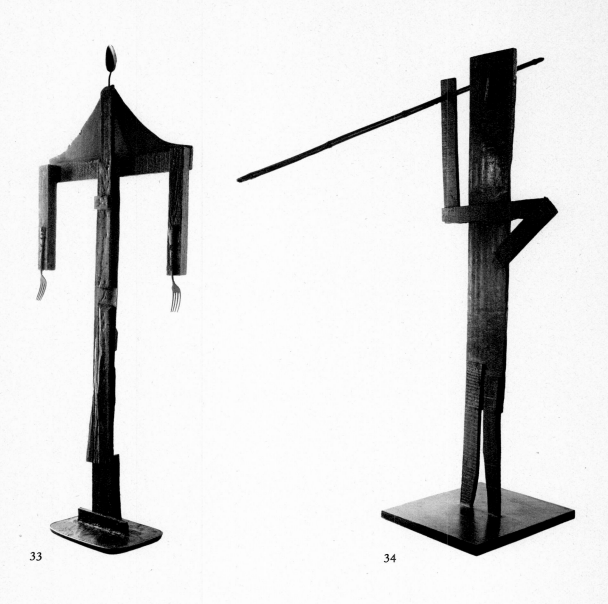

33   34

Standing Woman. Cannes, 1960. Bronze, 49¹/₂″ high.
Private collection, New York.

Standing Man. Cannes, 1960. Bronze, 48¹/₂″ high.
Private collection, New York.

35. *Arm*. Cannes, 1959. Bronze, 22³/₄″ high. Said
berg Gallery, New York.